When a Jew and Christian Marry

by
SAMUEL SANDMEL

♩ FORTRESS PRESS   Philadelphia

Copyright © 1977 by Samuel Sandmel

Library of Congress Cataloging in Publication Data
Sandmel, Samuel.
 When a Jew and Christian marry.

 1. Marriage, Mixed. 2. Marriage—Jews.
I. Title.
HQ1031.S26   301.42′9   77-78639
ISBN 0-8006-1311-2

6450E77   Printed in the United States of America   1-1311

Contents

Foreword

This book is for couples, where one of the two is Jewish, the other Christian, who have determined to marry, or have already married. How can they make a go of it? What are the possible pitfalls that can jeopardize such a marriage? How much does the religious difference mean? How much do family, history, and society intrude? What minimum ought the couple to know about Judaism and Christianity? In short, is such guidance possible as to insure a successful marriage?

Why this book? Such marriages have become frequent; it is asserted that one-third of all marriages involving Jews in the United States today are intermarriages. While this very bit of statistics is not absolutely verifiable, there seems no reason to doubt its general reliability. Indeed, those who express reservations about the statistics seem to feel that the figure is a bare minimum and should be larger. Accordingly, one can understand why there are those Jewish spokesmen who speak of intermarriages as the most important problem facing Jews in the Americas and western Europe. Some regard it as critical in its own way as the well-being or continued existence of the State of Israel.

Much that has been spoken and written about intermarriage reflects heat rather than light. Perhaps a deliberately calm exposition, even of what occasions and intensifies the heat, can possibly be useful.

Having written a number of books, I have had the experience of displeasing some people, even those who understood what I was writing. In trespassing into the delicate area of intermarriage, I am acutely aware of the likelihood of a misunderstanding of my purpose and motive. There will inevitably be those who will indignantly conclude my purpose is to promote intermarriage, and those who will conclude with equal indignation that I so stack the cards as to have written unreasonably and unfairly against intermarriage. Let me state, first, that I do not favor intermarriage, but rather counsel, in neutral situations, against it, because, among other reasons, I have the opinion that many people are unsuited or at least unprepared for it. But I repeat that the book is for those who have already made their decision.

There may be intermarried readers who have experienced a gratifying, successful marriage. Among them may be some who can say in fullest truth that they have encountered not a single one of the hazards the book sets forth. To those persons I would reply, first, that they are indeed fortunate, and, second, that I try to describe what intermarrying couples may encounter, not what they are certain to encounter. It has not been my thought at all that any one person would encounter all the negatives that I have assembled. The encounter, though, of even a fraction of them can be very disconcerting, or even shattering, if preparation and some advance understanding are fully absent. But preparation and understanding of problems do not eliminate the problems; the most they can accomplish is to assist in meeting them.

There are people who describe themselves as either Jews or Christians who are not so in any fervent way. They can be without any loyalty to or even identification with either Judaism or Christianity. There can, of course, be no conflict of loyalties where there are no loyalties. For such persons my book may seem totally dispensable. Yet, as the truism assures us, life can be full of surprises, and unsuspected loyalties crop up. So do unexpected problems and issues.

A person of an unwavering traditional religious bent could not have written this book. At the start I should make it clear that I am not at all an unwavering traditionalist. I subscribe to the view that religious traditions exist to serve people, not people to serve religious traditions. The welfare of a religious tradition can be different from the welfare of human beings. If matters come to the point wherein a choice has to made (and I cannot really envisage this), then I would put the welfare of people above that of even the most precious and admirable of traditions.

A word about the scope and purpose of this book. Because there is no dearth of materials which describe the religious life-cycle ceremonies, and the details of family or church or synagogue rituals and ceremonials, it is not the objective here to present these.

While many individual instances are on record which are examples either of the success or the failure of Jewish-Christian marriages, I have not felt that to provide a range of case studies was viable. Rather, the concern here has been to supply the general and basic material, with a particular emphasis more on the religious rather than the social issues. No book can offer specific guidance for each and every individual situation. This book is not meant to replace the direct counsel that some situations require. Surely some readers will want, and should seek, the guidance of their rabbis, priests, ministers, or marriage counselors.

I record my thanks to the Rev. Mr. Lowell G. McCoy, Father Reinhard Neudecker, S.J., and Rabbi Ronald B. Sobel for critical readings of the manuscript and for suggestions. The responsibility for the manuscript is, however, mine.

1

Social Backgrounds

Marriages of people of diverse national backgrounds have been common in the United States, involving persons of English ancestry, or French, or Scandinavian, or Italian, or Hungarian, and many others. The respective national backgrounds can be vivid if the participants are products of very recent immigration, or else be insignificant facts of family origin when the participants are products of an immigration many generations past. National origins tend to disappear in the progressive fullness of Americanization; the language is usually not remembered, and the characteristic food habits merge with hot dogs and hamburgers. Many Americans, indeed, are without keen awareness of or even knowledge of family origins.

Religious affiliation, on the contrary, is not a matter of the bygone past, but of its perpetuation into the present. An American of French Catholic origin ordinarily ceases to be a Frenchman but continues to be a Catholic; an American of Scotch Presbyterian origin ordinarily ceases to be a Scot, but continues to be a Presbyterian. Granted that facets of Christianity, especially Protestantism, have become greatly intermingled in America, religious affiliation, whether strong or weak, persists even when the national origins are totally forgotten.

When a Jew and a Christian marry, even if their respective religious affiliations are weak, the affiliations are not part of a half-forgotten past, but mark their living present. Diversity in religion, accordingly, is quite different in significance from that of national origin or other aspects of diversity.

In the United States, the religious diversity among Christians has left behind the wars, persecutions, and hostilities and theological quarrels out of which the vast array of

denominations came to be fashioned. The separation of
church and state, and the right of each religion to be freely
practiced, has produced a relative amity among the many
denominations. Indeed, there has been a broadly held view in
America that religion is an individual's private concern and,
moreover, all religions, so the feel has been, are pretty much
of the same quality. A Catholic Pope, Pius IX, in his *Syllabus
of Errors* of 1864, prohibited as a doctrinal error this view,
called by two synonymous terms, *indifferentism* and *Ameri-
canism.*

The religions in America perpetuate themselves in such
relative amity that we are startled when in our time violence
erupts between Catholics and Protestants in Northern Ireland.* Such violence is an unpleasant reminder to some
Americans of the sorrows of the past we have wanted to
disappear. In the relative amity in the United States, Jews
and Christians too have existed side by side in a way that has
drastically turned around their almost twenty centuries of
hostilities and mutual scorn, of persecutions and consequent
resentments. The age-old Jewish-Christian hostilities have
their origin in a complex religious difference without full
parallel in the arrays of other kinds of religious differences.

This unique religious difference led to consequences in
society, affecting Jews in matters such as civil rights,
economic opportunity, and daily life. Earliest Christianity,
before the word *Christianity* arose, was a Judaism; in time it
ceased to be that. In arriving at a sense of its discreteness, just
before 100 C.E.,* it was conscious of its Jewish origin, and
needed both to define it and also to express its justification
for having become a religion quite separate from Judaism. Its
justification included a basic criticism of Judaism and a harsh
judgment of Jews. These motifs were recorded in writings,
some of which were included in the New Testament and

---

*While the issues appear to be more political and economic rather than religious,
difference is in the background, and it is the religious difference which press and
television news reports stress, however unduly.

*C.E. is now the accepted abbreviation for *Common Era* and B.C.E. the accepted
abbreviation for *Before the Common Era.*

some which were not. The New Testament is the living heritage of Christians, central in Christendom today. The ancient motifs critical of Judaism and scornful of Jews are a portion of a broader Christian heritage, one of high-minded affirmations, profound theology, and lofty cultural attainments. A problem for modern Christians is the anti-Jewish motifs in the Christian heritage. While in New Testament books there are accounts of conflicts between Jews and earliest Christians and the Acts of the Apostles speaks of Jewish persecution of Christians, this latter is presented as sporadic violence, followed by intervals of amity. The Old Testament makes no mention of Christians, of course, for Christianity arose after that age. In the New Testament, however, Jews figure as hypocrites and villains, and Judaism is repeatedly presented as an imperfect or deficient religion. The problem of anti-Jewish motifs in Christian sacred literature is often abstract; perhaps it may be put in the following way: Can Christians become aware of, and come to terms with anti-Jewish motifs in its sacred literature in the light of its high-minded affirmations? In part the problem has been concrete, and arose from the reality that Christianity, on attaining power in the ancient Roman Empire, fostered and promoted disabilities and directed persecutions from which Jews suffered acutely. The disabilities and persecutions of the remote past can possibly be forgotten and disavowed as products of ages of cruelty and repression, happily behind us. But the anti-Jewish motifs in the New Testament are a portion of living Christian experience, and they trouble some Christians.

I shall return to this in the chapter which concentrates on the purely religious difference. Here I propose to deal not with religious doctrines but rather with aspects of sociology. It is a truism that people do not live in vacuums. There are in existence such things as Jewish communities and non-Jewish; Jewish social life, including Jewish clubs, and non-Jewish; Jewish philanthropies, and non-Jewish.

I shall try here to interpret to Christians what inner Jewish life is, and to Jews what the non-Jewish life is. In describing Jewish life, I fear that I shall have to list some grievances, especially if the occasion for them has passed. But to omit overtones of grievance, still alive among Jews, is to be false to the realities. Grievance leads to suspicion and distrust, and these are frequently latent factors in the Jewish mentality. Similarly, there is a frequent suspicion or even contempt for Jews in the Christian mentality, and such matters too will need some attention.

Intermarriage is possible only when there is some large measure of free encounter in society. Those who intermarry either are, or else think they are, free of the antecedent negative aspects of Christian-Jewish relations. But bride and groom and husband and wife have families and friends, and there are currents and cross-currents in society. Can an intermarrying couple cope with such things, either through creating a determined immunity, or else by facing their reality together, in full openness and understanding?

The currents and cross-currents we will look at will exhibit a wide range, running from ordinary strangeness through suspicion or condescension and reaching into marked intolerance and bigotry. It is not always easy to separate this range into neat categories.

What should a Christian know about Jewish experiences in the past century or century and a half? Many American Jews come from families which in Europe lived in bitter medievalism, even in modern times. Such families, on migrating from Europe, made a transition from medievalism to modern times in a journey that took only a few weeks. Medieval Jewish life was one of poverty and repression. It is summarized in the word *ghetto*, an Italian word of uncertain derivation. The ghetto was a dark, dank, undesirable part of a city or town where Jews were compelled to dwell. Their isolation was marked in several ways. Entrance to skilled trades and professions was barred. They were denied the opportunity for general education. They spoke not the language of the land, but a dialect of fifteenth-century High German. They had carried this language with them in the course of a combination of expulsions and wanderings. They wrote it in the

Hebrew alphabet. Its technical name is *Jüdisch-Deutsch*, which means the version of German which Jews used; its English name is *Yiddish*. Within the ghetto there was an inner life, centering in the synagogue, but there were also an array of buttressing philanthropic institutions which aided the indigent who could not afford the cost of a funeral or who could not provide a daughter with a bride's dowry. A school normally existed; its curriculum was the Hebrew prayer book, with which every male needed familiarity, and, for the few who could continue to study, the ancient rabbinic literature, compiled some fourteen hundred years ago (called the *Talmud*). Subjects such as mathematics or geography or history were not ordinarily taught.

In a large sense the ghetto civilization represented an ethnic entity, centered in religion but quite beyond synagogue devotional services. Europe, where national borders were often drawn capriciously, was host to a variety of ethnic groups resident in countries not their own, Germans in Poland, Poles in Bohemia, Yugo-Slavs and Serbians in the Austro-Hungarian empire. Jewry, especially in eastern Europe, constituted both a religious community and an ethnic group with a separate religion, separate language, and different culture.

Jews left Europe to escape poverty, oppression, and persecution. In colonial times there already were Jews here, though in small numbers. In the first half of the nineteenth century, the Jewish immigrants came mostly from western Europe, especially from Germany. In the latter part of the nineteenth century virulent persecution in eastern Europe prompted Jews in very great numbers to come to the Americas, especially to the United States; this large migration was renewed in the early 1900s when new persecutions arose.

Arriving here, Jews, of course, brought with them both their religion and their array of ethnic institutions and the memory of their sad experiences. Like other ethnic groups they tended to a natural gregariousness. Jewish food laws made it desirable to live near food shops that sold *kosher* ("ritually acceptable") food. Sabbath observance—traditionally using any means of transportation on the Sabbath is prohibited—made it desirable to live near the synagogues they built. Though free by law to live where they willed, Jews created voluntarily some aspects of the compulsory ghetto they had left behind. They established philanthropies, orphanages, hospitals, and other kinds of associations.

They brought with them, too, an ethnic sense, a strong bond born out of the common experience of repression and persecution. They brought with them the anxieties about what treatment they would receive from the world outside.

The process of Americanization is a matter often of the years involved in the adjustment to a new land, a new language, and a new set of circumstances. Immigrant groups have usually gone through the same pattern, of the foreign-born generation learning English while preserving the language brought along. The first American-born generation often understands the parents' language, although this generation, quickly learning an accentless English, veers away from the European tongue. The grandchildren ordinarily do not know the language of the the grandparents, though they inherit and retain some words and phrases or idiosyncratic expressions. Such words and expressions exist among Jews; some have made their way into American English.

For immigrating Jews there existed the desire to perpetuate their religion, and they could do this only be retaining a corporate identity. This has been the case, too, with other groups; for example, immigrating Greeks have had their wish to perpetuate their Eastern Orthodox faith. Jews, then, have deliberately preserved their religion. They have preserved aspects of their ethnicity not in the same deliberate way, but rather in response to how local situations have exerted pulls away from it. By our time, Yiddish has declined to the point of virtual disappearance, being confined now to very old people and to cities where there are many Jews. Food habits seem to be inherited; many a food shop, where three generations ago observant Jews bought their kosher victuals, has

become a gourmet shop where ancestral foods, and also forbidden ones, and other delicacies can be bought. In many an
American city a "Jewish center," a kind of YMCA or YWCA,
offers athletic outlets or a lecture series or facilities for a
"golden age" club.

That is to say, as Americanization proceeded, some facets
of the ethnic have disappeared, whereas others have not.

The gregarious instinct was in some ways balanced by outside pressure. For example, Jews have fashioned their own
social life. When they were able to afford it, they created
Jewish country clubs and Jewish college fraternities and
sororities. It came to be an American middle-class pattern
that, however abundantly Jewish and Christian children
played with each other at public school, or Jewish and Christian fathers saw each other at businesses or in the professions,
Jewish and Christian adults went their separate ways once the
business day was over.

This American-Jewish life has differences from the
European ghetto as well as resemblances. The differences are
exemplified in legal rights, for American Jews possess and
cherish American citizenship. Again, while at various times
certain vocational or economic outlets were tacitly barred to
Jews, hard work and thrift brought rewards, and a Jewish
pack-peddler speaking broken English, could found and
subsequently bequeath to his accentless son a tolerably
prosperous retail store, and a few Jews developed a retail
store into a large department store. Heavy industry, banking,
engineering, and university teaching were for a long time
beyond a Jew's attainment.

Hostility to Jews in the United States has been preached
by scattered bigots, and here and there a scattered act of
violence has taken place. Neither legal repression nor govern-
mental persecution has been experienced in the United
States. Two world wars brought Jewish and Christian service-
men, and their clergy serving as military chaplains, into close
relations, common military experiences, and common dangers in battle.

The social separatisms have at times been sharpened by the exclusion of Jews from clubs or resort hotels, and Jews have ordinarily chafed at such exclusion, but, accepting it, enjoyed their own clubs and vacationed at "Jewish" resorts.

Out of the circumstances so briefly outlined here, Jews have tended to be an "inner" group and the Christian world the "outsiders."

The ghetto life influenced the formation of a broad general mentality. The outsider, the Christian, was a persecutor; he was cruel, he was contemptuous of a religion which he deemed inferior to his own. All too often the Christians whom Jews encountered in Europe were illiterates; all too often these Christians were drunkards or beastly. It was a fact of life that "they" hated "us."

The American experience largely contradicted the European ghetto. Now Jews encountered genteel Christians, kindly Christians, Christians who seemed to have some respect for Judaism. There were, of course, Christians in America who were not genteel, and the social separatisms irked many a Jew, for he considered them to be gratuitous limitations on his freedom in society. Yet so relatively free from disabling barriers was America that by the 1920s, Jews, whose families had long been resident in the United States, had come to dilute their Jewish loyalties and weaken, or abandon, Jewish religious observances.

In the 1930s, Hitler came to power in Germany. At that time Germany was without question the leading nation in education and culture. German Jews had included eminent scientists, artists, composers; German Jews were quite proud of being German. Under Hitler, German Jews were forced to flee. If they did not flee, they were deprived of livelihood and possessions and were soon sent to extermination camps. The Nazi definition of a Jew was someone with one Jewish grandparent. This definition brought suffering and death to many a German who was only one-fourth Jewish; included as "Jews" were even Protestant ministers and Catholic priests. The Nazi definition of a Jew disregarded a Jew's loyalty or disloyalty to Jewish observances. The conclusion was natural that a Jew was inescapably a Jew, and subject to death, without regard to what he believed or did. Hitler, in conquering much of Europe, subjected Jews, whether in Poland or in France, to the same fate. One-third of the Jews then alive died at Hitler's hands.

Most Jews who were adults when Hitler came to power will never completely recover from the trauma of the Nazi period. It was a trauma even for those who, geographically remote, did not directly suffer the pains inflicted, the psychic terrors, or the ordeal of the concentration camps. Jews speak of the Hitler period as the *Holocaust*, a word derived from animal sacrifices found in various religious systems, meaning "totally burned," as were animals when offered on a fire altar. Our children, born after the Holocaust and hence personally not remembering it, seem often not to grasp the extent to which it was, and still is, a trauma to us.

It is not hard to understand how some European Jews, bewildered by an experience of horror that is unprecedented in the grim history of the persecution of Jewish people, saw all non-Jews as either the enemy or the potential enemy, and believe that safety and affirmative concern exist only in fellow Jews. That individual non-Jews, at great risk to themselves, hid this Jew or rescued that one, and that the people of Denmark, in a feat as spectacular as it was daring, saved the Danish Jews from the Nazis by carrying them by night to Sweden, could be noted and could elicit unreserved gratitude. Yet a broad sense that an outsider was a threat and a danger arose quite naturally. Many American Jews had relatives, including close relatives, in Germany and in the lands Hitler conquered. Here, too, disquieting developments appeared in the 1930s. A priest, Father Charles Coughlin, whose weekly broadcasts were punctuated by Nazi-like utterances, spoke over national radio every Sunday afternoon. An American Nazi Party arose. Some German-Americans established Nazi cells, replete with storm troopers, uniforms, and the Nazi symbol, the swastika. Some reflection of the European Jews' fears of outsiders arose among American Jews. Fear is instinctive, and a baseless fear is impervious to logic and reality. I do not recall that American Jews went into terror, but I do recall what one might call recurrent waves of genuine fear.

The Jewish religion has prohibited marriage outside the fold (as have some versions of Christianity). This prohibition, older than Christianity, is, accordingly, not focused on Christians, but is a prohibition of marrying outside the fold; it has its roots in passages in the Bible and has later been reaffirmed in ancient rabbinic legal codes. To this religious prohibition ethnic feelings and fears of the outside (accumulated over the ages) have added strong buttressing. A deep Jewish aversion to intermarriage developed and is preserved even today. The intermarrying Jew, accordingly, does something of which Jews collectively disapprove.

The precise nature or depth of this ancient disapproval is no longer uniform in American Jewish families. There are still some Jews who regard their intermarrying son or daughter as committing an act of betrayal of the gravest kind, to be marked by the need for observing the traditional rites of mourning for the dead. For such Jews, if the act of intermarrying is accompanied by the conversion of the Jew to Christianity, the bitterness of the sense of betrayal is the most extreme imaginable.

At another extreme, there are Jews who are unhappy at being Jews. The Jewish religion is meaningless to them. The burden of anxiety which persecution or discrimination has put on such persons is beyond their capacity to bear. They would often cease to be Jews, if only they could do so easily and comfortably, but they cannot, simply because of the entanglements of middle-class American society as has been indicated above. Such Jews delight in an intermarriage, possibly because a son or daughter may seem thereby to escape the burden of being Jewish, or possibly because they associate an intermarriage with some personal rise in social acceptability or status.

In between these extremes the ordinary Jewish disapproval

of intermarriage abides, yet with a range that runs from acute misery about it to discouraged and helpless acquiescence, the latter marked by the fervent hope that the marriage not turn out to be a mistake.

The Christian who marries a Jew needs to be aware of this aura of disapproval, and the reason for it, and, as it affects him or her, the subtle overtones of it. Such a Christian needs to grasp the character of Jewish devotion to Judaism and of Jews to each other, and to assess how he or she can respond to the status of being an outsider. He or she needs to understand the instinctive fears which Jews have had of outsiders as potential oppressors and persecutors, and that the family of the intended might possibly suspect even him or her of having this disposition or capacity.

If an intermarriage is to work out, then the Christian needs to understand that under discussion here is a general disapproval of intermarriage, and not a disapproval of the Christian as such. Naturally, there are circumstances in which a parent can disapprove of the person a child is marrying even if there is no religious difference. Such situations are not our topic. Assuming there is no personal disapproval, it is important for a Christian to understand that it is not his or her character or personality that is under question. Rather, he or she is a "dangerous" outsider. Perhaps disapproval is easier to bear when it is essentially impersonal. That Christian who is unable or unwilling to understand Jewish loyalties and anxieties sympathetically is scarcely ready to marry a Jew. Not even a Jew whose family is delighted that a child is escaping from the Jewish fold.

What the American experience has done for Jews has included a challenge to, or even abandonment of, the stereotype usual in ghetto society of the Christian as an illiterate drunk or a cruel monster. In free America too many Christians of education, culture, and generosity of spirit have come into the Jewish ken for that antiquated stereotype to exist in any vividness. Indeed, if it still existed broadly, then we would not have moved from the circumstance of two generations ago when Jews rarely intermarried to the circumstance today when intermarriage has become so common. But since it is a matter of record that Jewish laws have consistently prohibited marriage outside the fold, this prohibition—sometimes this one, and this one alone!—remains valid for many Jews while for others it does not. (Indeed some Jews are, curiously, unaware that the prohibition is explicit in ancient Jewish law.) There are Jews, accordingly, who regard intermarriage as a sinful trespass. My own impression, confirmed by rabbis who minister on university campuses, has been that most young American Jews see nothing wrong in an intermarriage, despite the traditional prohibition of it. There are those Jewish students who defend intermarriage as quite reasonable and proper, and those who sanction it as highly desirable. The age-old Jewish prohibition and disavowal of intermarriage, then, have significantly been repudiated by many young Jews. They normally admit, though, that the problem of family disapproval remains a reality and is something to cope with.

What should a Jew know about the Christian?
First and foremost, Christians are not an ethnic group in the sense that Jews are. Indeed, there are many, many varieties of Christianity, and Christians have not forged the unity that gregariousness, outside pressure, and the Jewish sense of community have among Jews. Some Christians belong to communions which do have a sense of community, but most do not. In any given city, there is in reality no Christian community as a balance to a Jewish community; there is, rather, a Jewish community set in a Christian world.

In the Christian experience in western Europe and America, it is essentially Jews and Jews alone who have been the non-Christians. The Moslem or Buddhist population in western Europe and America is numerically insignificant, and, if found at all, has made its way into the Christian world only recently. In the western world for countless centuries, Jews and Judaism have been the only non-Christian entity.

There is an axiom among committed Christians that Christianity is either the one true religion or at least the best of all religions. Phrases such as Christian charity or Christian love can be rendered as "the *best* charity," or "the *best* love." (Since the adjective *Christian* is meant to portray supreme approval, many a Jew has been spoken of in the United States as "the finest Christian in our community.")

Because Christianity arose in Judaism, Jews and Judaism figure in the Christian Bible; Christians and Christianity, of course, do not figure in the Jewish Bible.

A historic and continuing set of contradictions or ambivalences mark the Christian theological attitude to Jews. On the one hand, Jesus was a Jew, and so were his disciples. Moreover, God had "chosen" Abraham and his descendants, and Scripture speaks of the Jews as the "chosen people." On the other hand, the early Christian writings reveal that the Jews were blind to Jesus, rejected him, and charged with having "conspired" to have him crucified, an act for which they and not the Roman officials were the true culprits. Not only had the Jews of that time acted unworthily, but their religion had degenerated into a mechanical quest for material rewards. In Christian expositions, it is asserted that Christianity arose in a setting in which Jews had become unworthy and Judaism stagnant; it is set forth that the Christ had come in order to move a stagnant and deficient Judaism into its full perfection, for Christianity was the perfect Judaism. God, in bestowing perfection on Christianity, had chosen it to replace Judaism in his divine favor; he had chosen Christians to replace Jews as his elect people. Indeed, he had cast Jews off, whether permanently or for the interval of time in which the Gentile world would become Christian; at that future time God would return to the Jews. But until God would so act to save the Jews, they would remain unsaved, and therefore either they should be barred from society or else, if within society, be regarded as its pariahs.

The Jews, so Christians could concede, have possessed, as God's chosen, certain qualities which, in others, might be admirable. They have numbered good minds among them and people of some attainment. But the Jews, so ran medieval Christian thought, were in service to the devil, and in league with him, and hence their abilities were dedicated to nefarious ends. Or else a Christian in western Europe could, and did, reason in the following way: Jews alone resisted the Christian message, as if Christianity, while good enough for Gentiles, was not good enough for them. So great was the outrageous Jewish evil intention against Christians that they even scorned the figure of the Christ. Not only did they obdurately persist in not accepting him as the Messiah, but they even had the effrontery to deny that he was the true Messiah. They were not only non-Christian, but anti-Christian, and were probably engaged in plots to harm Christians. It was reported in the Middle Ages that Jews would sneak into a church and desecrate the holy elements of the Christian sacrament, or that they would kidnap a Christian child, kill him, and drink his blood instead of wine in observing the Passover Seder meal.

In modern times a Christian might reason as follows: Now that Christianity is split up into all sorts of sects, and the principle is to tolerate all of them, logically one should extend toleration to Jews too. But Christians cannot forget what Shakepeare taught, that the Jew Shylock is typical of all Jews in wishing for a pound of Christian flesh, or what Dickens taught, that Fagin, the master thief, was a typical Jew.

Or, one can hearken back to the Middle Ages before Christians found their way into decent banking. At that time, Christian rulers, needing financing, discovered that lending money at interest was forbidden Christians, but Jewish law allowed Jews to collect interest from Gentiles (but not from Jews). It was convenient to have Jewish money lenders in one's dukedom. In due course, however, Christians made money-lending respectable and there were some great Gentile banks established. But Jews have had a special gift for dealing

in money, and maybe the rumor one hears is right that it is
they who, today, really control the various money systems of
the world. (How false to the facts this latter is!)

And Jews (so some non-Jews seem to conclude) are something of an irritant in modern society. In the public schools,
for example, they seem to take it as an imposition on them
to sing the Christmas carols, and they mutter about the
separation of church and state, as if they think that there is
something religious about Christmas carols. If one gives a Jew
a job, he wants to be off on those silly Jewish holidays. He
stays on his job only long enough to learn the business, and
then he goes into the same line on his own, and this is in
some underhanded way, such as working nights and Sundays,
and he discovers how to undercut the Christian in prices and
services.

Let a Jew make a little money and he acts even worse than
other social-climbing *nouveaux riches*. Jews embarrass Gentiles in contributing to public charities, because they often
give amounts that are unseemly in generosity, and thereby
they either make others seem stingy, or else they impel Gentiles into gifts larger than they really want to make. So run
some frequent attitudes.

By and large, lower middle-class and upper middle-class
society differ from middle class, the extremes being marked
by a sense of security respecting their social position, for the
lower middle classes have no status to lose and upper classes
have no fear of losing status. But middle-class people who
yearn to be upper-class (as economic competency comes to
them) succumb to fears about personal prestige. If parents
are concerned that they must belong to the right country
club and must live in the right neighborhood, a prospective
Jewish son-in-law or daughter-in-law is a threat to the in-
secure status. This is especially the case where the parents
have bought a house they cannot easily afford, or joined a
club that is a tax on their budget, all in the hope that the
children will marry well. To have a Jew come into the family

can seem to defeat the purpose for which the parents ex
tended themselves or even made sacrifices.

By no means are all Christians hostile in ways here pointed
at. Rather in a broad sense there exists among Christians the
sentiment that for one's child to marry a Jew is the reverse of
a brilliant marriage, for brilliant marriages are to be found
only within the non-Jewish community.

The Christian who marries a Jew flies in the face of a
general Christian attitude of disfavor toward such a marriage.
Manifestly such a Christian rejects that attitude. But family
and friends may not.

Are there situations in which an intermarrying couple do
not encounter in their respective families narrowness, suspicion, or hostilities? Certainly there are such situations,
especially when the families have not been confined to the
social isolations which characterize middle-class America.
Yet, even in such favorable circumstances there are areas of
possible misunderstandings quite distinct from suspicion or
hostilities. The extent of escape from the past is often over-
estimated. To fall short of adequate understanding of the
past can readily lead to misunderstanding, and to minimize
the past, or to ignore it completely, is imprudent.

If the intermarrying couple lived alone on a desert island
there would not exist the prospect and likelihood of encountering the inevitable foibles and uglinesses such as the slur or
the insult in the careless word induced by too many cock-
tails. In my judgment, no Jew should ever marry a Christian
or a Christian a Jew unless each is purged of all possibility of
uttering a reproach of the other's religious background when
the inevitable tiff or passing quarrel arises. I have known
Christians who resent it when a Jew speaks of a damn *goy*, or
says, You're as stupid as all *shikses*.* I suppose the Jewish
sensitivity is even greater, when someone in anger says,
You're like all those damn Jews. People who speak this way
ought never, never marry.

*In Yiddish, a *shikse* is a Gentile girl, *shagetz* a Gentile boy.

How will the intermarrying couple respond together to matters more serious than bigoted slurs? To economic privation? To exclusion from a resort? To flagrant prejudice in the press? Fear is the inevitable result of bigotry and prejudice against Jews, but will a Christian married to a Jew feel that fear too? Or will the slurs reveal to him or her that the anxieties about marrying a Jew were not truly purged, but only suppressed?

Whoever marries out of the fold—outside his religion, his race, his nation, or his economic class—runs a risk.

The uniqueness of the religious differences between Christianity and Judaism, however, increases the risks. And for some men and women the dangers to a successful marriage are indeed insurmountable, especially if couples are over-optimistic and avoid speaking about what they need to explore in reasonable depth. The existence of attitudes on either side which includes feelings of inner superiority and a measure of contempt for the other may possibly be overcome more readily when brought into the open and discussed with reason and a degree of fairness. The greatest hazard lies not in the openly held viewpoints in the traditions but in the more subtle areas of unexpressed emotional identification and response. A Christian can learn the factual data about Judaism or a Jew those about Christianity. But unconscious loyalties that suddenly become awakened can present surprises which not only may be unpleasant, but be disruptive of a relationship.

2

The Wedding

Wedding plans too often provide the prospective bride and groom with encounters and confrontations which can be most disconcerting. Who is to officiate? A priest, a minister, a rabbi? Or a justice of the peace, or some judge?

Normally in American weddings a clergyman is desired. In some countries the law calls for a civil marriage, performed by an official of the government, and only after the civil ceremony does the religious ceremony take place. In the United States, individual state laws (the federal government does not enter into marriage) have the provision that a clergyman may legally officiate in lieu of the state. (Often a state law reads that a "minister of the Gospel" may officiate in lieu of the state, and by practice rabbis are deemed part of this category.)

If it is to be a clergyman, is it to be a Christian or is it to be a Jew? On what basis is the choice made? While in some instances the prospective bride or groom may have a strong preference, in many other instances it is the parents of one or of both who have a strong preference. Indeed, the tensions about the wedding arise from what in some cases, in effect, amounts to a family ultimatum, namely, that the wedding be Jewish, or the wedding be Christian. Such an ultimatum may carry with it the implied or explicit threat that unless a particular parental wish is complied with, disapproval to the point of a deliberate absenting one's self from the ceremony is to ensue.

In some circumstances there might be no strong preference on one side, with the result that the other side is more or less voluntarily granted its wish. If the respective parents have antithetical preferences, then embittered and embittering clashes may take place. The reason for this is that the question of which ceremony, the Jewish or the Christian, raises acutely the matter of loyalties, and therefore emotional adamancy arises. The couple finds itself harassed by desires or demands that are irreconcilable. One way out is for the wedding to be neither Jewish nor Christian by inviting a justice of the peace. To an adamant parent, however, that is no way out at all, for a civil ceremony can be as uncongenial as one in the "wrong" religion.

A second way out is to compromise by having both Christian and Jewish clergy officiate jointly. As we shall see, this possibility is ordinarily not feasible, though occasionally it is. Even when feasible, where adamancy exists this "solution" solves nothing.

Indeed, where adamancy exists the only solution is the capitulation of one side to the other. When bride and groom and their respective parents are unable jointly to come to some agreement, however reluctant, they are in for trying times and for utmost discouragement and frustration. In most cases, one side usually is persuaded to give in.

Perhaps a word of counsel might be useful here. The wedding ceremony itself (that is, if one does not count the music, the processional, and the recessional) is a matter of some ten minutes; the marriage in theory is to last a lifetime. In areas quite apart from religion, parental desires can conflict with the couple's wishes, for example, an elaborate, expensive wedding versus a simple one. Issues of this latter kind over the wedding are not worth fighting about, and it is better and wiser to give in to uncongenial parental wishes in such cases than to do battle over them, for it is the marriage, not the wedding, that should be of prime importance to the couple. Where this counsel is applicable respecting an intermarriage, I have no hesitation in urging it.

Let us assume, now, that the issue of who should be asked to officiate has been agreed on within the families, and the couple now approaches the clergyman. It is at this point that they encounter unsuspected shoals, especially if they do not understand what is at stake for the clergyman in officiating the ceremony.

To begin, a clergyman is always a member of some historic denomination and it is his denomination which has given him his credentials which entitle him to officiate. He is expected to abide by whatever commitments, tacit or overt, which he made when accepting the credentials at his ordination. His denomination has its own inheritance of beliefs and practices; these may include a prescribed wedding ceremony. If the ceremony which the clergyman is to use is prescribed as to content and form, a request that he deviate from it, or omit significant components, presents him with this issue: Does he indeed have the authority to deviate or omit anything from the service?

Inherited wedding rites almost invariably reflect the theological stance of the denomination, not just the personal views of the clergyman. To deviate or omit any part of the wedding service may present a clergyman with difficult questions beyond simply words, phrases, or sentences; the inherited prescribed ceremony represents a theological position he subscribes to. Hence, from the clergyman's viewpoint, it is reasonable to expect the couple which asks him to officiate to share in the theological beliefs of that denomination. One cannot reasonably expect a Catholic priest to officiate at the wedding of a Moslem to a Buddhist in a Methodist ceremony. There are subtleties of various kinds that arise when a couple of divergent religious backgrounds come to a clergyman of a particular denomination to be married. If the couple is ignorant of theology, or unconcerned about it, they will never grasp the very real problems many a clergyman faces when requested to officiate. The ideal situation is when clergyman, bride, and groom are fully in accord theologically; this accord would be assumed to exist without question when all three are antecedently of the same denomination. Where the clergyman and one of the marrying parties are of the same denomination, then it is usually assumed that it is the third party who will, or should, adjust to the other two. Such adjustment becomes possible through the "conversion" of the third party to the denomination of the other two.

We need now to modify matters a bit, without fully retreating from the content of the last sentence of the preceding paragraph. One modification is necessary respecting aspects of non-Catholic Christianity. In general, Protestantism, despite many inner differences, normally would not insist on precise denominationalism; that is, a Methodist minister would be apt to feel that no obstacles exist to his officiating at the wedding of a Methodist and a Presbyterian. To say this in another way, the criterion would not be the particular denomination within Protestantism, but it would be sufficient for the parties simply to be within Protestantism. Those Protestant churches which do not have a set liturgy ("order of worship"), such as Methodists, Baptists, Presbyterians, Congregationalists, Disciples of Christ would ordinarily set forth minimal requirements, if any at all. Indeed, many Protestant clergy will officiate at a wedding of a Protestant and a non-Protestant, or a Protestant and a non-Christian without raising any serious problems. On the contrary, churches such as the Roman Catholic, the Greek Orthodox, the Episcopal and some of the Lutheran churches, would ordinarily require the conversion of the third party to the church of the officiating clergyman.* The clergyman's response to an intermarriage is usually dependent on whether or not the church has a set liturgy which the clergyman would be apt to consider incumbent on him. If the intermarrying couple decide on a Jewish wedding (which entails a set liturgy), then the rabbi is almost invariably apt to require the third party to convert as a preliminary step to his officiating. A little later we will need to note that some rabbis, who represent Reform Judaism, are not stringent respecting required conversion.

---

*The key word is *ordinarily*. There are those churches which in recent times have been lenient respecting conversion; some stress, instead, the hope or expectation that children who will be born will be reared in the faith of the officiating clergy.

Perhaps it should be noted, for the clearest understanding of the problem that arises for the clergyman, that if his church in principle prohibits divorce, he would not and could not officiate at a marriage of two communicants of his own church if one of the pair has been married and divorced (unless the previous marriage can be declared to have been invalid). The point is that denominations have their historic rules and regulations and procedures about marriages, and a clergyman is apt to feel committed to these and lacks the authority to deviate from them.

The word *conversion* is used among religious people in two senses. Some Protestant churches mean by conversion not moving from one denomination or one church to another, but rather a step beyond by which a person changes from mere formal adherence to a conscious, willed, and decisive adherence. Such churches, accordingly, do not mean by conversion a shift from one denomination to another, but only a shift in what we might call the character of one's adherence within his church.

When conversion is taken to mean a shift from one religious communion to another, it is a usual supposition that while ultimately the convert will make an internal decision and thereafter go through some rite or ceremony, he must first undergo instruction. The purpose of such instruction is to insure that the convert understands the principles of the communion he is entering. The premise is that he cannot, and should not, go through the conversion rite until he has mastered at least the basic theological teachings, for understanding must preceed the will to convert and the act of conversion. Roman Catholicism and Judaism have in common that a prospective convert must first undergo instruction. Many nonliturgical Protestant churches have little or nothing required in the way of formal instruction, but put the premium on the will and decision of the would-be convert.

Catholic priests and rabbis are disturbed by an implicit anomaly, namely, that there are in both communions faithful individuals who know little or nothing in depth of their tradi-

tions. So to require the outside party to undergo instruction
can bring about the situation that the would-be convert is
knowledgeable far beyond the party born either Catholic or
Jew. Some priests and rabbis therefore require the born
Catholic or Jew to undergo the same instruction as the convert.

Once the convert has been deemed adequately instructed,
he can then be received into the church or the synagogue by
a profession of his adherence to its doctrines. The usual
Christian rite is baptism. Among traditional Jews, male circumcision is part of the process; for women converts to
Orthodox or Conservative Judaism, a ritual bath (which Jews
never call baptism!) is a requirement. Reform rabbis usually
do not require male circumcision or the ritual bath.

Are some things peculiar or even wrong about conversion?
The answer is yes. For example, one must ask the question
about motivation and goal. When conversion is for the sake
of satisfying the demands or wishes of a family, is it for its
own sake (as purest sincerity should imply) or is it for what is
in the final analysis the result of an ulterior motive? How
earnest can a conversion be when it aims at satisfying situa-
tional demands? It is part of traditional Jewish doctrine
(scarcely heeded today) that conversion in connection with a
wedding is unacceptable since, in such cases, an ulterior
motive is the real purpose.

Again, how can one decide what quantity of instruction
constitutes an adequate amount? Five sessions, or ten, or
fifty? Over how long a period, days, weeks, or months? Whatever answer is surely a matter of some subjectivity or even
caprice. Moreover, what is the precise relationship between
whatever facts may be absorbed through instruction and the
inner transformation which conversion implies? Is a profession of adherence to the new faith adequate if it is only a rite
and recital of a formula? Is formal conversion a matter of the
heart, and long-lasting, or is it only a useful expedient?
Experience would suggest that conversion for the sake of a
wedding is often only an external accommodation.

In the case of the conversion of a Christian (a genuine

one!) to Judaism, or a genuine Jew to Christianity, much more is entailed than the mere absorption of factual data. We must later look into this at some length if we are fully to grasp what this means.

Are there matters related to intermarriage which are quite beyond satisfying the demands made by the family? Suppose that a justice of the peace officiates at the wedding, or that a clergyman is available who is willing to officiate with no future religious commitments required, or that a wedding takes place where there has been no conversion, i.e. the Christian remains a Christian* and the Jew a Jew. How divisive is a divided home?

Obviously, the more sensitive and considerate the couple are to each other, the fewer are the tensions that can arise, and the easier it is for the tensions to be handled. There seem to be some instances in which such an arrangement of non-conversion, with each partner abiding in his own religion, apparently works out quite well. This is especially the case where the marrying couple is of an age beyond child-bearing. An inner understanding seems to operate here, at least between the two.

But where there is the expectation of the birth of children, the possible tension is greater. Not that hostilities necessarily arise. It is, rather, that it is quite difficult, and in many cases impossible, to rear children in both Judaism and Christianity. I know of instances in which exactly such an effort is made, and of families which, in conformity with this goal, observe both Christmas and Hanukkah, Easter and Passover. I know of one instance where there were many children; the parents reared the first· third, and fifth as Christians, and the second, fourth, and sixth as Jews; I have heard such parents boast about how well it is all working out. Perhaps that is the case. Or perhaps the parents desperately wanted it to work out.

A somewhat more frequent arrangement is to rear the

---

*It is possible in these days in Roman Catholic procedures for a Catholic to receive a "dispensation from the form" of being married in a church, and he may thereafter be married in a synagogue or court without losing his Catholic status.

children in no religion whatsoever, on the premise that this arrangement provides a strict neutrality on religion; it is assumed, or stated openly, that the children at maturity will choose which religion they want. Granting earnestness in such situations, I believe it true that the parents have really made a decision for their children against religion, for in abstaining from any religion, they have in effect preconditioned their children to none. If it is the ultimate desire of the parents to want to obstruct their children from religion at maturity, that is fine. But it is my conviction that the choice of no religion is a wrong one. It is much sounder and wiser to rear children within a religion (and at maturity they can make a choice to continue or not to) than to withhold them from it.

Another arrangement is to abandon both traditional Christianity and Judaism and to join a church or fellowship which seems to be neither one nor the other. The Unitarian church is often chosen. While in New England (and elsewhere) the Unitarian church seems to remain Christian, as it surely once was, outside New England it often proclaims itself as non-Christian. Local Unitarian churches often become havens of refuge for those who no longer feel at home in traditional Christianity, and in recent decades homeless Jews have found it attractive. Often the Society of Friends, especially the Hicksite (that is, a modernist form) version of Quakerism, seems as neutral as Unitarianism. I have a deep personal admiration for both of these "fellowships." My halting reservations have to do with my perception of both the Unitarians and the Friends as meeting some of the intellectual demands of intelligent people, but not the emotional yearnings innate in most human beings. These two communities seem to be subject to the circumstances, even in situations where there has been no intermarriage, that people seem to drift out of these fellowships as casually as many drift in. Profound adherence, with all one's mind and heart and soul, seems regrettably elusive. Perhaps that is why these highly praiseworthy fellowships have never grown beyond pitiably small aggregates, numbering a few hundred thousand (Unitarian-Universalists 400,000, Quakers 100,000) in a country of over two hundred million. The adverse judgment I am here venturing to express is that these fellowships do not adequately satisfy what many or most people seem to want from a religious denomination.

If for most people there seems no viable choice but conversion, then one must in all frankness say that earnest conversion is exceedingly rare, for all too often the mind is quite willing but the heart is not. This is quite normal, for it is easier to learn the academic lessons that instruction demands than to break ingrained associations. I do not think that it is too hard for a Christian to learn that Jews will not attribute special divinity to Jesus or, for that matter, to Abraham, Moses, or Isaiah. But Jesus is quite as much a matter of feeling as of thought. The words and phrases of childhood become second-nature to all of us and for a Christian to speak of "our Lord Jesus Christ" is so deeply ingrained from childhood that it is to expect a great deal, perhaps too much, of him to desist from those words. Or, if he can desist from such words, it is even more difficult to rupture the sense of spiritual unity that exists between a Christian and the figure of Jesus. I do not think that it is too difficult for a Christian converting to Judaism to learn that he must hold that Jesus was only a man, and not more than a man. To suppose that such learning will disengage him from the innate, spontaneous association of Jesus with all that he holds precious is perhaps to expect too much. In my experience, few ordinary Christians are able to explain in ordinary terms what Jesus signifies to them, and even fewer can give a coherent explanation of what the term *Christ* means. I do not think that such inabilities are at all relevant, or that they go to the heart of the matter. Rather, "Jesus" is a way of Christian feeling, a means of expressing what would otherwise be inexpressible. There is for Christians something thoroughly appealing in the figure of the babe in the manger and of the mature figure who went to his death on behalf of humankind. The cross, or the crucifix, speaks to Christians with an eloquence that words never succeed in achieving. To suppose that a Christian can renounce so profound a feeling seems to me to be highly unlikely. Yet, it is precisely this which a conversion away from Christianity would require.

Similarly, I am sure that an ordinary Jew, wishing to convert to Christianity, can quickly memorize the Apostles' Creed. He can learn that in a traditional marriage ceremony he is expected to kneel (something Jews never do in a synagogue) and he can comply. The recurring phrase, "Father, Son, and Holy Spirit," of the Christian ceremony should at least in principle be, or become, as precious to him as to a Christian; that is to say, he must move from either lack of acquaintance and exposure (or even a scorn of the phrase) into an affirmative and sincere alignment with it, as if it is directly meaningful to him. So, too, the allusions to "our Lord Jesus Christ" ought now mean to him *his* Lord Jesus Christ. But it is much easier to speak such words as a formula than to mean them earnestly. A sympathetic recognition on the part of some Christian clergy of the inordinate difficulty involved in a transition from merely saying these words to meaning them leads some to a willingness to omit them, because the clergyman considers them either "offensive" or at best meaningless to a Jewish sensibility; in such a case the clergyman either directly on indirectly interprets the phrases as only rhetoric, as a Christian way of speaking, and presumably he thinks that behind the words there lie basic religious ideas common to Christianity and Judaism. Some Christian clergy, however, are quite justified in feeling that if the wedding is a Christian wedding, then it ought to be Christian in its entirety. But whether these phrases are omitted or included, it ought to be clear that some tension, emotional rather than intellectual, attaches to them. As I shall point out in greater detail later, there is a great gap between a view of Jesus as a man, admired completely without reservation, and Jesus Christ as one's Lord and Savior. A Christian wedding centers not in the man Jesus, but in Jesus as Lord and Savior.

Surely if the wedding ceremony does not reflect the true convictions and heartfelt assent of bride and groom, but only appeases adamant relatives, it is perfectly legal, yet something of a sham. I have known grooms and brides for whom the sham of the wedding was the regrettable but chief recollection of it.

The point of all this is that full and earnest conversion is rare. Quick conversion, after a few easy lessons, often meets the demands of a situation. But the lifelong relationship that ought to mark a marriage can easily be threatened by later reflection or second thought, especially when a couple come to realize that they have had recourse to what has been only a mere convenience. The seed of bitterness is all too often sewn, and the harvest of a resentment of implied or open coercion can jeopardize the marriage. Where conversion is merely a form or a convenience, the bride and groom, in having recourse to it, ought to know what exactly they are doing, so as to forefend against a later disproportionate regret.

There is often an aspect of a conversionless wedding in connection with which the officiating clergyman stipulates as a price for his officiating the commitment, oral or written, that the couple's children be reared in his communion. (Some churches ask not a *commitment* but an earnest promise, or even a signed declaration, to live by the faith, and to do all in one's power to try to rear the children in that church.) It ought to be recognized that such a commitment, declaration, or promise, assuaging the conscience of the clergyman for officiating where he may not really feel at ease is, in effect, a forced compliance; it is a promise or commitment made, whether in good faith or not, as a means of getting out of immediate problems. I have reservations about the reliability and desirability of promises exacted by force and I fear that such promises are either completely worthless or else not worth very much. Whether the promises are lived up to or not depend on the life-style of the bride and groom after their marriage; I doubt that such promises or commitments strike the couple as truly binding on them.

Certain clergymen feel that the personal conscience is more important than the traditional demands of the denomination, whereas others in the very same communion will insist on all the traditional demands. Accordingly, two different couples in fairly identical circumstances may discover that two clergymen in the same communion may respond antithetically, the one in an accommodating, elastic way and the other, courteously or rudely, in an unaccommodating way.

In one type of proposed arrangement—a joint Jewish-Christian ceremony—the couple ought to expect a range of possible responses by clergymen, running from an absolute refusal to take part in any joint officiating to a ready willingness to do so. Very often the contrast of willingness and unwillingness about joint officiating is quickly characterized as a difference between a broad, liberal clergyman and a narrow, bigoted one. Why do I assert that it is not a matter of breadth or narrowness? Because, at least in my own understanding, the authority of a clergyman derives from the credentials granted him by some historic church. An ordained Catholic priest is not a Methodist minister or a justice of the peace and ought not to act as other than a Catholic priest. A rabbi is not an Episcopalian priest or a circuit judge and ought not to act as other than a rabbi. I know of an instance of a rabbi officiating at the wedding of two "homeless" Christians (should one say "ex-Christians"?); in my judgment, this rabbi was acting beyond his due authority and exalted as were his motives) he was abusing it.

Let me here become personal as to what I feel I can *in conscience* do, and not do. I am a Reform rabbi. The only ceremony I feel I have the right to use is that in the Manual of Reform Rabbis. Since I am a professor, not a congregational rabbi, the invitation to me to officiate at a wedding of even two Reform Jews is a rarity, perhaps twice in a span of three years. The invitation to officiate at an intermarriage is even rarer. My own practice, if one can use this word in the light of the infrequency of my involvement, is to give the bride and groom a Xerox of the wedding service in the manual. I ask them to study this service; if it is agreeable to their consciences to be married in such a service, they can extend their invitation to me. If this service is not agreeable to their consciences, they ought not to invite me. They make the basic decision, not I.

Do I require instruction and a formal conversion? I do not. I require only that they assure me that in clear conscience they can be married in the only ceremony I feel I have the right to perform. Can this arrangement in its own way be a sham, kindred to that in convenient conversion? I suppose so. I simply believe that an appeal to conscience is superior to a set of prescribed demands. I firmly believe that the learning of data flows more readily and voluntarily out of conscience than out of the compulsory prescription which a course of instruction involves. Naturally, I want some time to be spent in a frank and as thorough as possible inquiry into both the service and its implications. Certainly one implication is that the couple are throwing in their lot with each other, the Christian with the fate and welfare of Jews, but I do not ask for an advance commitment about how the children will be reared. What is done with the children should flow naturally and in due course from the implications, rather than be an advance coerced commitment. I concede that my procedure has the overtone and nuances of a conversion to Judaism, but surely it is quite different both from a requirement of instruction and examination, and also from a formal rite of conversion. I personally shun such rites, and have been a party to it in connection with a wedding only once, and that was some thirty-five years ago. That conversion took place on the eve of the wedding (at which another rabbi, not I, officiated). At the reception following the wedding the very next day, the bride, having drunk a bit more than was seemly, confided to me in a loud voice, and a four-letter word, what a farce the conversion ceremony had been.

To my recollection, I have participated in a total of three other formal conversions. In the first, the convert had been married to a Jew for many years, had reared the children in the synagogue, and at the occasion set for the formal conversion which she wanted, one of the three rabbis, the usual number in a formal rite, was unable to attend because of illness; I was telephoned some ten minutes after the appointed time for the ceremony and was asked to substitute, and I was willing to do so. A second instance was in Germany, where the wife of a Jewish serviceman had satisfied the required instruction and had already fully identified with the Jewish community, and the two chaplains of the area wanted me (I was there to lecture) to serve as the third rabbi; I did so. In the third instance, a wife, who had thoroughly identified with her husband's synagogue, where their children had been reared, was about to undergo serious exploratory surgery and wanted her formal conversion to precede her entry into the hospital. In all three instances, the formality of conversion was a sequel, and not a convenience in advance of a wedding.

I do not, then, regard the formality of conversion as qualifying or disqualifying. It can be a meaningful gesture, a milestone step which can gratify a person, and if meaningful to that person, it can and should take place.

If a Christian is prepared to throw in his or her lot with his or her Jewish mate, and this in the fullest sense, and if the two can in good conscience be married in the only ceremony I feel able to use, then, I am prepared to officiate.

While state laws, to repeat, grant the rabbi the right to "officiate,"—in the historic Jewish sense—the rabbi does not marry the couple, but rather they marry each other in the presence of the rabbi. It is not the rabbi's personal or inherited, corporate beliefs that are of the essence, but rather those of bride and groom.

There is a place at which, though, I personally draw a line. Since I will not deviate from the only service I feel qualified to use, it follows that I cannot be a party to what has twice been asked of me, namely, to participate in a joint Jewish-Christian ceremony. Perhaps my unwillingness is vestigial anti-Christian bias, but I do not think so. I simply do not

know how a joint Christian-Jewish order of service can be
concocted, and have both Christian and Jewish authenticity.
The response could be made, and I have heard it, that the
presence and participation of a Jewish rabbi and a Christian
clergyman supply these ingredients. Perhaps. My own perception is that such a service is neither one nor the other. I have
heard people who have witnessed such ceremonies speak
glowingly of their beauty and harmony. I can only say that I
could not take part in such a service for it would violate my
conscience. There are other functions in which clergymen
participate where I in conscience will not. I will not give a
benediction or invocation at a public meeting, especially at
banquets of nonreligious community organizations. Football
fan that I am, I have said no when asked to say an invocation
at a football game. It is my idiosyncrasy, then, not to participate in a Jewish-Christian wedding.

I do not feel the same way about a funeral, for a funeral
service does not put the clergyman in the situation of serving
in lieu of the state. I have officiated at a simple service of a
non-Jewish friend who had no religious affiliation. I would be
willing to share such a service with a Christian clergyman, in
the hope that the anomalies would be at a minimum.

One more word. Is a joint Jewish-Christian wedding service
the product of a decision? Or is it in essence a token of the
deferment of basic decisions? The wedding ceremony takes
about ten minutes. Will a lifelong marriage endure when
decisions are deferred and evaded?

A couple determined to have a joint Christian-Jewish service will encounter reluctance or refusal, especially from
most rabbis. If they are diligent in their search, they will
ultimately find acquiescent clergymen. But let them know
that they can expect some measure of refusal and that they
should be prepared for it. They should know that what they
are asking for is irregular, while the refusing clergyman is
sticking to what is regular.

I have learned to my dismay that in certain very large cities
there is an occasional rabbi who traffics in intermarriages,

asking and receiving exorbitant fees for officiating. To my mind this constitutes a reprehensible betrayal of principles. I scorn such rabbis. I pity those Jews who have so little aware-ness of the nature of Judaism that they utilize such services. What is left of the sanctity of the wedding ceremony if the officiant makes a business of it?

3

What a Christian Should Know About Judaism

I fear that all too often an intermarrying couple restrict the religious difference to the figure of Jesus. How wrong this is! And how unrealistic it is to suppose that if the Christian chances to be one who is not a traditional, literal believer in the divinity of Jesus that the religious differences are thereby dissipated; they are not.

What in the main should a Christian know about Judaism, and a Jew about Christianity? And what are the possible tensions? We begin with the important introductory statement that since Christianity originated in Judaism, the two traditions have many religious words in common. Not only do they understand these words in different ways, but they ascribe different values and importance to them.

Basic to Judaism is its sense of history. Long, long ago, so runs Jewish belief, God chose his people, as it is recorded in the Book of Genesis. The people originated from an ancestor, Abraham, in a line through his son Isaac, and Isaac's son Jacob. In turn Jacob (also known as Israel) had twelve sons, each the ancestor of twelve tribes which comprised the "sons of Israel." In the time of Jacob, one son, Joseph, through a series of events, became an official of the highest importance in Egypt, with the result that his father and brothers all settled in Egypt, the welcome guests of the Pharaoh of the time. Thus a family clan of some seventy souls increased in Egypt into a "nation," to which the Bible ascribes the figure of 600,000 souls, apart from women and children.

Under a new Pharaoh, the children of Israel were enslaved and oppressed. Through God's intervention, and the great leader Moses, they were redeemed from slavery, and they left Egypt, with their destination the land Canaan which God had promised to Abraham for his descendants. (The Greek word for that land was *Palestine*.) But prior to the journey to the land, Moses led them to the sacred mountain known both as Sinai and Horeb, where great events took place: God revealed himself to the corporate people for the fashioning of a "covenant," a contract, between God and his people. The covenant demanded of God that he protect, defend, and lead his people; it demanded of the people that they be faithful to God by shunning the worship of any other deity and by obeying an array of laws, foreshadowed by the Ten Commandments, which would soon be revealed in abundant detail through Moses and his brother Aaron. Yet even as God was graciously revealing his will and laws to his people, they turned to making and worshiping a golden calf, thereby incurring divine wrath and divine punishment. This momentary but extreme infidelity was overcome, and Moses then proceeded to have artisans make the religious paraphernalia to be housed in a portable sanctuary which was suitable for the Wilderness. The movable sanctuary was destined to give way to a permanent one when once the people would have settled in the land, and fully possessed it. Through Moses, an annual calendar of sacred days was provided; a system of animal sacrifices was enjoined; a hereditary high priesthood was established through the installation in that office of Aaron, the brother of Moses. The priests were a clan within the tribe of Levi; the eldest son of the high priest was to inherit that office from his father. One function of the priesthood was to preside over the rites of atonement, a process by which restoration to good standing could be achieved in the event of "sin." By sin was meant an act in intentional violation of those revealed laws, which were the content of the covenant. Such a violation could be by an act of commission or of omission. The Hebrew term for the aggregate of revealed laws and of accompanying divine exhortation is *Torah.* By extension, the word *Torah* came to mean the Five Books of Moses (Genesis, Exodus, Leviticus, Numbers, and Deuteronomy).

The range of topics in the Torah goes far beyond the narrow confines of what we today ascribe to religion, for the

Torah includes laws relating to manslaughter and murder, theft and burglary, usury, and slavery. That is to say, the Torah includes as of the same religious character what we would tend to separate into the categories of civil and religious law. Some of the laws of the Torah are for the individual, some for the corporate people of Israel. Some deal with purity and impurity, as related to personal hygiene; some deal with permitted and prohibited foods. In principle, then, the religion of the Torah encompasses all aspects of life.

The holy days were prescribed as part of an annual calendar of recurring events, involving the priests, the Tabernacle (and later, the Temple), and the people. The system of restoration from sin centered in two sacred occasions, and the intervening days, the "ten days of penitence," beginning with *Rosh Hashanah* (New Year Day) and culminating ten days later in *Yom Kippur* (Day of Atonement), the latter a fast day. Three festivals were designed as "pilgrim" occasions, pilgrim in the sense of entailing obligatory travel to and attendance at the Temple in Jerusalem. The first of the three, *Sukkot* (Booths), a fall harvest festival and the ancestor of the American Thanksgiving, derived its name from the use in its celebration of a rude structure of branches and boughs of trees, this in recollection of the temporary lodgings used by the Hebrews in the Wilderness journeys on leaving Egypt. The spring festival, *Pesach* (Passover), commemorates the redemption from slavery in Egypt. Ten plagues had been visited on the Egyptians, the last one entailing the marking of the homes of the Israelites so that God could "pass over" these homes and confine his dire punishment to the Egyptians. Also, the haste of the Hebrew departure from Egypt is commemorated by a special bread, free of yeast and of rising, hence flat cakes, called *matzoth;* there was no time when the Hebrews fled Egypt to wait for the bread dough to leaven and rise. The third festival, *Shavuot* (weeks) comes seven weeks after Passover; a spring harvest festival, it commemorates the momentous events of Sinai. The Greek word *Pentecost* ("fifty") was used in later times among Greek Jews as their word for *Shavuot* (the day comes 49 days after the second day of Passover, and hence 50 days after the first day). The three festivals were in principle to be celebrated by attendance at the Temple in Jerusalem, but buttressed by home observances.

A recurrent weekly day of rest, the *Sabbath,* falling on Saturday, required a complete cessation from all work (including such activities as cooking, travel, or carrying packages), and was obligatory on all men, women, and children alike. The account of creation in Genesis tells that after the six days of creation, God himself rested on the Sabbath.

The Torah, then, ascribed to the Wilderness period the establishment of a divinely revealed legal system, encompassing all aspects of living, and an elaborate worship system, primarily animal sacrifice, for the moment assigned to the portable Tabernacle but eventually to be centered in a permanent Temple.

The Wilderness journey was to culminate in the entry into and settlement in Canaan, the land divinely promised to Abraham. But even during the Wilderness wanderings, it became clear that peaceful entry and settlement would be resisted by the Canaanites by a show of force. The land therefore needed to be conquered and its inhabitants overcome.

The anxiety that future contact with Canaanites would lead to religious contamination led to the divine injunction that the Canaanites be completely exterminated. The conquest of Canaan took place under the successor to Moses, Joshua. A tricky maneuver by the Gibeonites, a Canaanite people, spared them from general extermination, with the result that Canaanites persisted in the land. The period of settlement was marked by wars with both Canaanites and neighboring peoples. Moreover, religious anarchy prevailed at the time, known as the age of the "judges," and the view arose that only through the rise of a king over all the twelve tribes would this anarchy be eliminated. While in the Wilderness period God had spoken directly to Moses, his will in the times after Moses was revealed by certain spokesmen or "ser-

vants" he designated, called prophets. The selection of the
king was God's responsibility; he disclosed his choice by
having a prophet anoint (pour oil on) the designated man;
such a monarch was deemed "God's anointed," for which the
Hebrew word is *mashiah*, in English spelled "messiah." Historically, the first king was Saul, duly anointed by the
prophet Samuel. But Saul's evil deeds in time disqualified
him as king; at God's behest Samuel anointed Saul's successor, David. With David a whole dynasty was born. David
was not only a warrior, but also a musician-poet, and to him
were later attributed the poems in the Book of Psalms.

His son Solomon was privileged to build the permanent
Temple in Jerusalem, in replacement of the portable Tabernacle of the Wilderness period. Solomon was a sage, a wise
man, to whom were ascribed the Book of Proverbs (as well as
Ecclesiastes and Song of Songs). But Solomon married many
wives, including Gentile women, and they were responsible
for defiling the purity of the exclusive worship of God. As a
consequence of this defilement, punishment came in the
reign of Solomon's son Rehoboam. The northern tribes broke
away from him, rejecting the dynasty of David, and forging
the so-called northern kingdom of Israel. Rehoboam and his
descendants continued to rule over the southern kingdom,
with its two tribes, the small tribe of Benjamin and the large
tribe of Judah, whose name was given to the southern kingdom.

The age of the monarchy is known to us from the Books
of Samuel, Kings, and Chronicles, and from the writings of
prophets such as Amos, Hosea, Isaiah, Micah, Zephaniah, and
Jeremiah. The legacy of the literary prophets is a constant
reminder to Jews of the fidelity due to God, of the dire
consequences of infidelity, and of an unreserved concern for
ethics, the latter deemed to be the concrete aspect of fidelity.
Moreover, the prophets were concerned with what the flow
of time meant, and what it was that lay ahead for the people
in the future. The general view was that God had a purpose in
the events that were taking place, especially in the actions of

the kings, and also that neither king nor people ought to obstruct God's purposes. History, so the Hebrews believed, was moving towards a goal of universal justice and peace, and kings and people came under judgment respecting their conformity with God's revealed purposes towards that goal.

The northern kingdom of Israel was conquered by the Assyrians in 722-721. Its population was moved out of the land eastward and there absorbed; in popular lore, these tribes who had disappeared became the "ten lost tribes." The southern kingdom lasted until 597 when it was conquered by the Babylonians. A rebellion in 587 led to the destruction by the Babylonians of Solomon's Temple; in its wake the court and the leading citizens were moved eastward, to exile in Babylonia. Unlike the Israelite exile, the Judahites retained their identity in Babylonia. While the affection for the "Promised Land" did not fade away, the essential bond now came to be the relationship between God and his people, wherever his chosen people happened to be.

When the Persian, Cyrus, conquered the Babylonians, and the Persians dominated that part of the world, the exiled Judeans were allowed to return to their land. They rebuilt the Temple. No new king arose; instead, Judah (or, to use the Greek form of the name, Judea) was governed by the high priest. The Torah presumed to have been revealed in the Wilderness and written by Moses became the "constitution" by which the Judeans lived. We can speak of this as "biblical religion," especially to differentiate it from what was later to ensue. It was a religion of social ethics with its worship at the Temple centering in animal sacrifice, accompanied by psalms, and presided over by hereditary priests under the leadership of the high priest. At some point in the period after the return from Babylonia, the Five Books of Moses became a required subject of common study and knowledge. The spoken language changed from Hebrew to Aramaic, and a knowledge of Scripture included the need to translate from Hebrew to Aramaic. Also, attendant challenges to understanding arose, especially of matters dealt with in the Bible only briefly or by implication. Places of study in local towns slowly began to arise. Yet the center of the religion remained in the Temple, with its system of animal sacrifice, and its inherited priesthood, as prescribed in the Bible.

In 332 B.C.E., Alexander the Great conquered the Persians, and Palestine became part of his world empire. He died in 323. In the division of his empire among his generals, Judea fell under the sway of the Ptolemies of Egypt, though claimed by the Seleucidians with their capital at Antioch in nearby Syria. On the one hand, Greeks colonized Judea through their merchants and their founding of Greek cities. On the other hand, Jews now voluntarily spread throughout the Mediterranean lands. They settled in very large numbers in Egypt, especially in the thriving city of Alexandria, named for Alexander. Alexandria in many ways was the New York City of the ancient world. Some seventy-five years after Alexander's death, the continued loyalty to Judaism of Egyptian Jews led to the translation, about 250 B.C.E., of the Five Books of Moses into Greek. This act of translation underscores a subtle change that was underway, in that a sacred book, the Bible, was arising to broaden the center of the religion, first supplementing the Temple, sacrifices, and the priesthood, and later rivalling the Temple. Also within Judea, and, indeed everywhere that Jews voluntarily scattered, Scripture became the primary focus of their Jewish loyalty.

The requirement of fidelity to God became a critical issue in Judea as a consequence of the acute intrusion of Greek culture around 175 B.C.E. Though Judea had been ruled by the Ptolemies of Egypt, by legacy from the time of Alexander, it was claimed by the Seleucidians, who about 198 took control of it. Judea was caught between the Seleucidians and the Ptolemies because geographically it lay between them. Not only had the Greek language become frequent in Judea, but Greek institutions such as Greek temples and the theater were found in the land. In Jerusalem, there were some Jews who outraged others by openly adopting Grecian ways, including undergoing a surgical operation to remove the sign of circumcision. These hellenizers (adopters of Greek ways) appear to have come from the upper classes and to have included priests. The power of the office of high priest included a lamentable series of ugly rivalries for the position, and some trafficking with Greek authorities for appointment to the high office and the retention of it.

The issues between the Seleucidians and the Ptolemies led to some events of critical importance to Jews. The Seleucidian king, Antiochus IV Epiphanes, returning to Antioch after an incursion into Egypt, outraged Judeans by plundering the sacred Temple. Then, faced by uprisings in his eastern domains, Antiochus sought to be free of challenge in the west by seeking to enforce a religious uniformity, and as a consequence, attempted to destroy the Jewish religion. Rebellion against him, led by a family called both Hasmoneans and Maccabees, erupted in 168. Some three years later, the Maccabeans were able to capture the Temple and to "purify" it; the rededication is still observed by Jews in the festival of *Hanukkah* (rededication), which falls near Christmastime. A confused period of guerilla warfare against the Seleucidians, who were beset by a succession of kings and struggles for power, eventuated in the recognition of Jewish independence. A Maccabean dynasty arose, first as high priests and then as kings.

But as significant as the regaining of political independence and a dynasty was the slow growth of religious impulses in areas away from the Temple and centering in Scripture. The local places of the study of Scripture became places of prayer. For such places of study and prayer, both Hebrew and Greek names have survived, the Hebrew words being *house of study* or *house of gathering*; the Greek word is *synagogue*.

The word *synagogue* relates to Judaism by association, and not by the inherent meaning of the word. It had two senses, one, the simple act of assembly, and, later, the place where the assembly took place. At first, then, a synagogue was not a building, but rather only a gathering of people, as in a home, to study and pray.

It is thus possible in the Maccabean age to speak of beginning "synagogue Judaism" as something distinct from the Judaism of the Temple, the animal sacrifices, and the priests. Biblical injunctions provided that there be only one Temple, in Jerusalem; a synagogue could be anywhere. At no time, anywhere, were animal sacrifices ever offered in a synagogue. The leadership of a synagogue was not by hereditary priests but by ordinary laymen. Gradually, as study moved more and more into prayer, the beginnings of a rudimentary order of worship arose, destined later to become relatively fixed, enlarged, and extended through the use of biblical readings, especially more and more psalms, and even newly-devised prayers not excerpted from Scripture. Quite as significant as the new mode of worship was a growing array of religious doctrines and practices not explicitly found in Scripture. In the realm of law, where Scripture is either brief or general, logical deduction led to new formulations, often limited to "clarifying" Scripture, but just as often suggesting innovation. In the realm of thought, there had arisen in portions of the populace a view about the fate of a person respecting death. Was death the end of a man? Or was there perhaps an afterlife? Usually traced to Persian influence, the concept of "resurrection," meaning that though an individual died, he would be restored to life at some due time in the future became important. In the realm of Scripture study, questions of all sorts could be raised quite naturally. For example, Scripture tells nothing about the boyhood of Abraham, yet would not a student of the Bible wonder what kind of a lad he was? One might find the suggested answer in some word or phrase of Scripture, and then proceed to tell a tale about Abraham, who as a boy chopped to pieces the wooden idols in the idol shop his father owned in their native Ur. Such a tale about the boy Abraham could lead to still another and yet another, not simply for the sake of a good story (many are very good!), but to make some ethical or religious idea vivid. Still another form of study was recourse to the use of a parable, a short anecdote which, by using the form of narration, had a force beyond mere abstraction. (Here is a parable on mutual responsibility: Three men owned a boat in common. When they were in the middle of a deep lake, one man suddenly produced a drill and began to bore a hole. Chided by the other two, he responded, "This is my part of the boat." [Most of the parables in the synagogue study were about kings].)

The total process of deriving laws and of telling vivid stories was dedicated to the purpose of making Scripture, already a very ancient book, relevant to the new times. Because the new, derivative laws and the vivid exhortation were intimately associated with Scripture, there arose a view to justify a union of that which was new with the very ancient Scripture. That view was that when God had revealed to Moses in the Wilderness what he was to *write* in the Five Books of Moses (which Jews call "the Torah," the revealed law and instruction), he also revealed to him what he was to *say* to his associates and his followers, and these oral words of Moses were transmitted from generation to generation. There was, then, so it was held, a double legacy, the written Torah, recorded in the Five Books of Moses, and the oral Torah, new laws and exhortation passed on by word of mouth, but ultimately deriving from Moses.

The requirements in the written Torah, since they reflected God's revealed will, required full compliance. The general principle of protection to ensure full compliance with these laws became known as the "fence around the Torah." It consisted of instituting a new, derived law in order to ensure the full and precise fulfillment of the biblical law. To use a modern example, let us assume that a mother, entrusting her children to a baby-sitter, says, "Do not let them play in the street." The baby-sitter, to reinforce the mother's law, tells the children, "You may play only in the back yard; you may not play on the front sidewalk, or in the front yard."

The Judaism of the synagogue developed and adhered to the protective principle respecting biblical law through "a fence around the law."

Manifestly, some derivative laws are *not* explicit in the Bible. Hence, a "sect" called the Sadducees arose whose attitude was that only what is explicit in Scripture, that is, the written Torah, is true Torah. The Sadducees thus denied the authority or aptness of the oral Torah. They appear to have been an upper middle-class group, who found the observances in the Temple and a literalistic approach to Scripture sufficient for them. The Pharisees, essentially of middle- or lower-middle class, fostered the oral Torah, that is, the oral as well as the written Torah. It is usual for scholars to associate the Pharisees with the synagogue and with a freer, more elastic approach to Scripture than the literalism of the Sadducees.

If the essential distinction between the Sadducees and the Pharisees was religious, there were nevertheless echoes of various rivalries for power and influence in the course of the Maccabean dynasty, including Pharisee-Sadducee rivalry. Internal disorders, spurring local insurrections, impeded tranquility, and hence the later Maccabean rulers were inclined to petty despotism. But the petty turned into the serious and the acute about 65 B.C.E. when a younger brother of the legitimate heir to the Maccabean throne tried to supplant his older brother. Rome had a presence in the east by this time. It intervened in 63 B.C.E. to seize control of Judea and to end its full independence. Now internal strife involved pro- and anti-Roman sentiments and uprisings. The Romans ended the limited Maccabean rule by designating a certain Herod to be their "client-king," this in 40. In 37 B.C.E., Herod actually came to the throne; he ruled with the support of Rome and also with his own unique despotism and cruelties. During his lifetime the land seethed with unrest against both him and Rome. He died in 4 B.C.E., the year in which the birth of Jesus is usually believed to have taken place.

At Herod's death, his kingdom was divided among three

sons. One son, Philip, is of little concern in subsequent events. A second, Herod Antipas, was appointed tetrarch (equivalent to duke) of Galilee, the northern area where anti-Herodian and anti-Roman activities were frequent. A third, Herod Archelaus, became king of Judea. Protests against him led the Romans to depose him, and they governed Judea from 6 C.E. into the sixties (except for an interval from about 39-42) by a succession of Roman procurators (governors), the best known of which was Pontius Pilate (26-36), during whose term the career of Jesus occurred.

Constant uprisings, cruelly repressed, led to open revolt in Judea in 66. Initial Judean successes were soon reversed. The Romans destroyed the Temple in 70, and crushed the last rebels in 73.

The destruction in 70 brought an end to the Temple religion with its sacrifices and its high priest and subordinate priests. Jews have offered no animal sacrifices since that time. Synagogue Judaism was by now already on the scene.

Judaism has survived only in the form of Synagogue Judaism. In many senses the Judaism which a Christian encounters in our time is essentially the Synagogue Judaism of long ago.

Its main characteristics ought here to be summarized. Synagogue Judaism is essentially a layman's institution. Its preoccupations are with prayer and study. A national judicial body, the *Sanhedrin* (this Greek word means "congress"), was in existence before the age of Herod, and apparently dissolved, to be revived under a courthouse after 70. In local situations smaller, restricted courts flourished. There slowly emerged the office of *rabbi*. The word means "my teacher." The rabbi was a teacher of the Torah, and partly a lawyer and partly a kind of judicial figure. He was necessarily an expert in Torah, both the written and the oral. What the rabbi was *not* is also important to notice: he was not a synagogue functionary, and did not become so until the nineteenth century. At some point, hard to pinpoint, rabbis supplanted the

Pharisees in the synagogue leadership. If very early Synagogue Judaism might be called Pharisaism, after 70 C.E. it is
more appropriate to speak of Rabbinic Judaism, rather than
Pharisaism.

The nub of Rabbinic Judaism is fidelity to the two Torahs,
fidelity to the specified requirements both of the written
Torah and the derivative laws of the oral Torah. In the view
of Jews, these laws *in principle* have never been abrogated or
cancelled. The observance of the laws is possible only if one
knows them; hence among Jews a good minimum of education, at least by males, has always been obligatory.

What are some additional characteristics of Synagogue
Judaism? One characteristic is its sense of logic, its conviction
of its rationalism. Granted that Scripture provides accounts
of miracles, by and large the tradition has believed in the
essential rationality of its convictions. The conformity
demanded of Jews was that of observance, not that of doctrine in any great detail. To deny either the existence of God,
or of God's rule, was abominable atheism, but obligatory
belief did not normally extend beyond that one item.

Where in the view of Synagogue Judaism was history leading? A future of great promise lay ahead, this in sharp contrast with the dismal present, marred as it was through the
domination of the foreign power of Rome and its incivilities,
marred by poverty, crime, and unrest, marred by the way in
which the collective people lived, not in peace in a land of
milk and honey, but rather dispersed throughout the then-
known world. Surely an age destined to come in the future
would replace this age of evil. When? When, at long last, God
would judge the world, both nations and individuals. When
would that be? In God's own time, probably in the remote
future, but possibly it might come soon, suddenly. If that
moment was long delayed, then there was a temporary
release for an individual, that is, in his death, for he could
then promptly enter into the world to come, already available in heaven, and there await the climactic events of the
future when they came. What would mark this climax? The

coming of God's anointed, his messiah. Such an agent of God would surely some day emerge! He would destroy the power of the foreign conqueror, and either designate a Jewish king, or, as some thought, himself be that king. Who would he be? Someone fully suitable for royalty, and therefore someone definitely not a Maccabean or a Herodian, but rather a descendant of King David. At his wondrous coming, Satan's grip on this world would be broken, allowing God's kingdom to come. At that auspicious time, God's judgment day would be inaugurated, and either all men would be resurrected and judged, or else all men would be judged and the righteous resurrected. At that glorious time the dispersed of Israel would be miraculously transported back to the now glorious land of milk and honey. Yet quite possibly the new era could dawn only if the present age became even worse. Surely, though, God would prepare his people for the great day by first sending to them the prophet Elijah who had not died but who, at the close of his career, had ascended to heaven on a pillar of fire. Yes, first Elijah would come to prepare the way, and then the Messiah would miraculously appear. Yet men should be on guard against conscious or unconscious deceivers who falsely claimed to be the Messiah.

The faithful needed to give attention both to what the laws required and to the question of how to observe the laws. The "how" involved both the procedures, which needed to be defined with exactitude, and also the motives of people, for though reward attended him who faithfully observed the laws, one's motive in fidelity should be conformity with God's will and not simply an expectation of reward, or its opposite, a fear of punishment. Each man was free to choose whether to observe or not to observe, for even though God's providence ("foresight" and "concern") led him to watch over men and guide what happened to them, providence did not extend to the point of denying one's freedom to choose, or the moral responsibility for the choice he made.

Moreover, the collective people were the people of God,

bound to each other both by ties of blood through a common descent from Abraham, but also by the ties that shared suffering and recurring hopes arouse and cement. Proselytes and converts were welcome, provided their motives were pure, and provided they were prepared to share in the so often unhappy lot of collective Israel.

That ancient Synagogue Judaism, as I have said, is by and large the Judaism of today. Certainly it went through development, as, for example, the refinement of the meaning of certain doctrines through the work of medieval philosophers, and through the elaborations and acute definitions of Jewish laws through a sequences of "codifiers." A movement arose in the eight century called Karaism; it was a "back-to-the Bible" movement, with its adherents denying the validity of the rabbinic laws. Even today tiny pockets of Karaites still exist. The Karaite movement, once significant in numbers and influence, serves best to underscore the continuity of modern Synagogue Judaism with the past.

In our time we encounter terms such as *Orthodox, Conservative*, and *Reform Judaism.* These terms need explanation, but one should beware of explanations which rely too heavily on modern Christian counterparts, for the analogies can be as misleading as they are enlightening. Moreover, the range of modern Judaism is scarcely exhausted by the words Orthodox, Conservative, and Reform, but, as we shall see, needs to include partially observant Jews, and nonobservant Jews, and Jews who are Jews only by accident of birth.

The distinctions presently to be set forth will be essentially those of basic philosophy. Let us understand, however, that in reality very few Jews are keenly aware of these underlying philosophical distinctions. For example, it is not by philosophy that Jews differentiate Orthodox, Conservative, and Reform, but by external manifestations, exemplified in the contrast between the practice of Reform Jews to pray bareheaded and of Orthodox and Conservative Jews to pray with head covered. Hence, I must give two sets of distinctions, the one philosophical, the other practical.

Orthodox Judaism is in principle a direct and unaltered

continuity with the ancient Synagogue Judaism. Its guides
are the oral Torah, which, paradoxically, came to be
recorded; the classic book or the oral Law is the *Talmud*
("learning"), a two-part work. The first part, the *Mishnah*
("teaching"), is a recording made between 175 and 200
B.C.E. of the oral Torah, in "tractates" arranged on the basis
of topics (Sabbath, New Year, Divorce, and the like); the
second part, *Gemara* ("deduction"), is a compilation of
rabbinic discussions of the Mishnah, recorded between 450
and 500 C.E. (and inherited in two varying versions, one
from Palestine and the other, and more frequently used, from
Babylonia). Later codifiers did yeoman service in introducing
better order and system; they wrote works of such erudition
and utility as to become useful, authoritative, and handy
compendia. The best known is the *Shulchan Arukh* ("the
table is set"), the guide book most often used by Orthodox
Jews.

The basic premise in Orthodox Judaism is the eternal
validity of the Jewish requirements and the doctrines recorded in the ancient documents. The next sentence is of
prime importance: *authority in Judaism resides in the ancient
documents, and nowhere else.* By nowhere else, I mean that
Jews have never had a pope, or a world ("ecumenical")
council of official individuals who, alone or in assembly, constituted an authority more or less equal to the authority of
the inherited written word. Here and there an individual
rabbi, or regional council, achieved a status of some authority, but only in a transient or local sense, and he could not
transmit his authority to someone else. What this means is
that practices such as, for example, not riding on the Sabbath
remain since Orthodox rabbis cannot arrogate to themselves
the authority to change the inherited laws. In a sense, then,
Orthodoxy in principle is totally committed to "no changes."

Reform Judaism is a product of the eighteenth-century
rationalism, and the social upheavals such as the French
Revolution and the toppling of the ghetto walls. In the realm
of philosophy, Reform is kindred to "modernist" Protestantism, representing an effort to adjust the doctrines of tradi-

tional Judaism to the modern age. It accepts the results of biblical scholarship; it interprets resurrection to mean immortality, thus denying physical resurrection; it substitutes for the personal messiah of traditional Judaism the hope or expectation that society, through a blend of God's guidance and man's achievement, will some day achieve a messianic age of universal peace and well-being. In the realm of synagogue practice, Reform Judaism abolished the seating of women separate from men (traditionally women occupy either the balcony or, if there is none, a curtained-off section) and reduced the length of the worship service by eliminating some prayers and shortening others. It sanctions the use of the language of the land in place of the traditional Hebrew. It abolished the requirement of a *minyan*, a minimum quorum of ten males, traditionally the hallmark of a proper public worship. Whereas in the traditional synagogue the expenses for light and heat were met by selling, even at auction, certain privileges presently to be mentioned, Reform introduced annual dues, systematically handled by mailing out bills. In a Reform service, the Torah continues to be read out of a parchment scroll as in Orthodoxy, but it is *read*, whereas in the Orthodox synagogue the assigned reading would be chanted. Instrumental music, prohibited in an Orthodox synagogue, is permitted in the Reform service, and an organ (to some Orthodox Jews a clear symbol of Christianity!) is usual. In Reform, a mixed choir is usual, whereas in an Orthodox synagogue a male soloist would be unaccompanied; such a singer is called a *chazan* or cantor. In the United States and Canada, the males pray bareheaded in 98 percent of Reform synagogues, whereas in the Orthodox synagogue, the males would wear a skull cap, for which the Slavic word is *yarmulke*, but this word is giving way more and more to a Hebrew word, *kippah*. In Orthodox worship, the males wear a *tallit* ("prayer shawl"); in Reform worship the tallit, if worn at all, is worn only by the rabbi (and cantor) in the pulpit, seldom by those males in the pews.

A distinction, seldom fully expressed, exists in the basic

WHAT A CHRISTIAN SHOULD KNOW ABOUT JUDAISM   59

approach to the rites and ceremonies. In Orthodoxy, these are regarded as divinely enjoined, while in Reform they are regarded as symbols. A result of this distinction in basic approach is the difference between the Orthodox regard for punctiliousness in the observances, and a lack of punctiliousness in Reform, and, indeed, as indicated, the Reform abandonment of some observances. An Orthodox Jew does not write or ride on the Sabbath, or light a fire, or flick an electric switch, considering such things as prohibited because they are work—the ancient definition of work was a pursuit by which one earned his livelihood. Reform Jews do not observe such prohibitions. With respect to dietary laws, one might speak of the written Torah which prohibits the eating of pork and shellfish, and the oral Torah which prohibits the eating of meat and dairy foods at the same meal; in connection with the latter, Orthodox Jews maintain two sets of dishes and kitchen utensils, one set for meat and one for dairy products. With respect to permitted meat and fowl, the word *kosher* (ritually acceptable) goes beyond the food itself, and relates to the manner of slaughter by a trained functionary called the *shochet* (ritual slaughterer) and extends to the requirement of salting permitted meat long enough for all the blood to be removed. (The word *kosher* as applied to pickles is singularly inappropriate; it is used to describe a pickle as prepared in European Jewish communities and transported to the United States and called *kosher* by very generous extension; in this latter sense, kosher simply means "prepared as Jews have prepared them.") Orthodox Jews will not eat prohibited foods, or mix meat and dairy products together, nor eat from dishes or utensils not separately guarded by strict observance.* Reform Jews in general do not observe the dietary distinction between meat and dairy foods, and I suppose that most regard the biblical prohibitions as no longer binding; Orthodox Jews will not eat in a

*A Christian can be assured that it is no great burden to live by Orthodox regulations. The rules can easily be learned by any person willing to learn them. A Christian should know that Orthodox Jews take such regulations in stride, needing to give them no undue attention.

restaurant which is not kosher; Reform Jews will. Orthodox
Jews maintain a rigorous fasting on the Day of Atonement,
while Reform Jews include many who fast, though not as
rigorously (the Orthodox fast begins late in the afternoon
and lasts all night and all day until evening stars appear; the
Reform fast begins after evening has set in and lasts through
the afternoon worship); some Reform Jews do not fast at all
on principle. In observing the pilgrim festivals and the New
Year, Orthodox Jews maintain an additional day which was
added in the ancient rabbinic age, while Reform Jews have
dropped such added days. A day in Jewish reckoning runs
from sundown to sundown; the Sabbath eve synagogue worship in an Orthodox synagogue begins at sunset (and thus
may be as early as 5 P.M. in winter or as late as 9 P.M. in
summer daylight time); the ordinary practice in a Reform
synagogue is to adhere to a set hour, like 8:00 or 8:30 P.M.
Thus, the Sabbath eve service in an Orthodox synagogue
precedes dinner; Reform innovated an after-dinner "late" service.

Conservative Judaism arose essentially in disapproval of
the "extremes" of Reform. It is marked by some moderate
borrowings from Reform, for example, the late Friday night
service, and some use of English, especially for the sermon,
but is generally in principle as traditional as Orthodoxy. In a
loose way, Conservative Judaism lies in between Orthodoxy
and Reform in its theory, but in synagogue practice Conservative is closer to Orthodoxy than to Reform.

But in our time a Christian marrying a Jew will encounter
a welter of confusions which are the result of what I earlier
called partial observance or nonobservance. There are Jews
who belong, in deepest loyalty, to Orthodox or Conservative
congregations and who would oppose tampering with the
synagogue worship, but their private lives are marked by
partial or even nonobservance with respect to the dietary
laws or riding on the Sabbath. Some nominally Orthodox and
Conservative Jews maintain their homes in a strict kosher
way, but eat in restaurants; some who eat in restaurants will

order only fish, beef, or chicken, but some will even eat
prohibited foods. In a sense, the words *Orthodox, Conservative,* and *Reform* are clues to which synagogue a person
affiliates with, and not to his practices.

The confusions are even greater. Today, a distinction is
necessary between Orthodoxy, strict Orthodoxy, and strict-
est Orthodoxy, for Orthodoxy in itself is a composite of
varied degrees of traditionalism and diversity. In our time,
virtually all Reform congregations have veered towards traditionalism by the reintroduction of ceremonies which earlier
Reform had abandoned. On the one hand, one can in our
time encounter Jews, generous in Jewish philanthropies, and
even leaders in Jewish organizations, who boast of no synagogue affiliation, or brag about their lack of observance of
usual Jewish sacred days or customs! On the other hand,
there are Jews who are dues-paying members of both a
Reform and an Orthodox synagogue, and some even of a
Conservative synagogue in addition. In the United States it is
usual for the Reform synagogue to be called a temple (as is
the case with a few Conservative congregations), though it
must be clearly seen that a Reform temple is a synagogue and
not a temple (which, as when mentioned above in connection
with the Temple in Jerusalem was a place of animal sacrifice)
at all.

Why these anomalies? Because modern life in general, and
American life in particular, is conducive to them. There are
Americans who call themselves Christian who never trespass
into a church or subscribe to a Christian creed. In the case of
Jews, there is a sense in which to be Jewish is every bit as
much ethnic (as implied in Chapter 1) as it is religious. Little
that I have observed in Jewish college fraternities or Jewish
country clubs justifies the adjective Jewish except that the
members are Jews *ethnically.*

Yet nonobservant as such "ethnic" Jews may be, they can
be marked, either voluntarily or by reaction to various
external pressures, by a latent loyalty which manifests itself
in ways often surprising. One can encounter an emotional

aversion to a child's marrying a Christian as strong in a non-observant Jew who believes in nothing as in an earnest Orthodox Jew for whom such a marriage is religiously prohibited. Irreligious Jews demand that a rabbi marry and bury them!

It is usual for a Christian to discover a great array of Jewish organizations besides synagogues in even a city of moderate size. They include a "Jewish Center" with activities to appeal to varying age groups and interests. Jewish women are to be encountered in Hadassah (a Zionist group), Brandeis women (for the support of Brandeis University, which is a secular university that marshalled financial support from Jews), the Council of Jewish Women (often concerned in areas similar to that of the League of Women Voters), and dozens more. Men are to be found in the B'nai B'rith (a cultural and philanthropic group). Often there is a Jewish hospital (whose patients are usually more than 90 percent non-Jewish). Various charities have local chapters, as do so-called defense agencies (which I discuss in Chapter 5 on Anti-Semitism). The local charities find an overall unity in a "federation," which is, in turn, usually part of the general, city-wide United Appeal. The overseas charities are usually constituted in a Jewish Welfare Fund. There is often a consultative council composed of representatives of the various local organizations called the Council on Community Relations. That is to say, there is no dearth of Jewish organizations quite apart from those normal to a synagogue.

Instruction for children is mostly the responsibility of synagogues. There are, however, special city-wide Jewish educational enterprises, usually for a stress on instruction in Hebrew. In many places there is a partial or a full school, communally supported, which Jews are apt to call an "all-day" school, deliberately shunning the Christian word *parochial*; the all-day school is usually Orthodox in direction and disposition.

Perhaps what should emerge above all in the perception of a Christian is the essentially pragmatic characteristic of Jews.

Ideology and theology are relatively latent, and seldom explicit. The Jew who belongs to a particular congregation makes his choice on the basis of his sentiment about traditionalism, not on any analysis of the theological stance (that is, do the males wear the yarmulke or not, rather than, What does Orthodoxy or Reform hold theologically?). Jews have been taught to have a special responsiveness to the charities, and an adulation of education. It is necessary to say that in our times Jews have an extraordinary high number of people well educated in the disciplines of the university, but their education in Judaism is scarcely at the level of children; in short, Jews are usually as illiterate about Judaism as Christians are about Christianity.

4

What a Jew Should Know About Christianity

What should a Jew know about Christianity and Christians? Perhaps, first and foremost, that the loyalty of a Christian to Christianity is apt to be no less intense or exalted than that of a Jew to Judaism.

The Christian Bible both overlaps the Jewish Bible, yet is different from it. Most Jews know that the Christian Bible includes the New Testament, which of course, is absent from the Jewish Bible. There are also two differences respecting what in Christian terminology is known as the Old Testament: first, in some Christian communities the list of books in the Old Testament is longer than the list in the Hebrew Bible, because Greek Jews bequeathed to Christians some books which they had adopted as holy. Accordingly, some Christian communities, such as the Roman Catholic, have in their Old Testaments books such as I and II Maccabees, the Wisdom of Solomon, Ecclesiasticus, Tobit, Judith, Esdras, and additions to the Books of Esther and Daniel. Since the sixteenth century it has been convenient to allude to these additional books by the term *Apocrypha.* In some Christian communions the Apocrypha have the same sanctity as other books, but in others they are regarded with less than full sanctity.

Second, the arrangement of the order of the books is different. In the Jewish Bible there are three sections: first, the Five Books of Moses; second, the Prophets; and third, the heterogenous "Writings" (Psalms, Proverbs, Job, and the like). In the Christian Old Testament, the literary Prophets come third, not second, so that one can turn one page, as it were, from the last lines of Malachi with its prediction of the return of Elijah, to the Gospel of Matthew in which John the Baptist is, broadly speaking, identified as this Elijah. Jews and Christians, then, have a common legacy in what Jews call Bible and Christians call Old Testament. Later we will notice that this common legacy is interpreted in quite divergent ways.

Historically, Christianity is the child of Synagogue Judaism, not of the Temple. It is the child of ordinary, humble Jews, not of the Sadducean aristocracy of Jerusalem. Many Christians have little awareness of this. Also, they are prone to regard Jesus not as the Jew he was, but as so exceptional as in fact to have been virtually not a Jew at all. It is the rare Christian who is prepared emotionally to view Jesus in his Jewish context, and this despite Christian scholarship and textbooks which stress his Jewishness over and over again.

Why is this so? In part it is explainable in the way in which the figure of Jesus has been transmitted in Christian lore, whether in Christmas carols or in the more formal instruction in church schools. Christians have strong emotional ties to the Gospels, kindred to the ties which Jews feel for the Torah. In the New Testament there are four Gospels, and these are the principal sources for knowledge about Jesus. Bits of additional information about him are found in New Testament writings such as the Acts of the Apostles, an account of Christianity in the decades immediately after the time of Jesus, and in letters written by Paul of Tarsus. Normally Catholics and traditionally-minded Christians speak not of Paul but of *Saint* Paul, and not of other early personalities as Peter or John, but as Saint Peter and Saint John; many modern Protestants are inclined to omit "Saint."

What do the Gospels tell and what do they not tell? They tell about those things Jesus did, and about his teachings. They do not tell enough about him for a full or even nearly-full biography, nor do they provide any generous quantity of background material. They assume on the part of a reader a general acquaintance with Synagogue and Temple Judaism, but make no effort to provide full detail.

There are in the Gospels, as in books of the Hebrew Bible,

passages that are less than clear. There are also, as is the case in the Hebrew Bible, passages which conflict with other passages. Some materials in the Gospels are regarded by modern Christian scholars as legendary, or in other ways lacking in historical accuracy (as we understand historical accuracy today). The view exists among most New Testament scholars that the "Jesus of history" cannot be recaptured; it is among trained scholars, and not among usual Christians, that this view exists, and a Jew errs if he attributes to his Christian in-law the skeptical views about Jesus he may have gained from a scholar in a college course.

Certain external facts about Jesus are widely agreed on. Jesus was born, in all likelihood, in 4 B.C.E. (If it is asked, how he could have been born in the period B.C.E., the answer is that when a sixth-century Christian historiographer made an effort to equate Roman and Christian dates, he made an error in equating them.) Some Christians, however, believe that he was born in the year 6 C.E. When did he die? The Gospels give no exact date, but it was in the term when Pontius Pilate was governor of Judea (see above, p. 53) which lasted from 26 to 36 C.E. A passage in Luke (3:23) speaks of Jesus as thirty years old; another passage (John 8:57) speaks of him as nearly fifty. Modern scholars usually ascribe the death of Jesus to 29 or 30 C.E.

The Jewish title *Messiah* is attached to Jesus in the Gospels. That Hebrew word, when it is translated into Greek, is "Christ."

The Gospels may rest on documents that were written in Hebrew or Aramaic, but none of those documents have survived. The Gospels are in Greek, and most scholars agree that they are not translations into Greek, but were written in that language. The four Gospels in the New Testament are named for the traditional authors; on the basis that a common content and purpose animate the four, each is known as *the* Gospel, but there are appended to "the Gospel" the words *according to Matthew, Mark, Luke,* and *John.* Modern scholars list the chronological order of the Gospels as follows: first Mark, then Matthew, then Luke, and finally John. No passage within a Gospel gives a date when it was written; modern scholars *usually* ascribe Mark to the period around 70, Matthew 80-90, Luke 85-95, and John 90-100. (Some individual scholars follow their own bents and supply quite different dates.)

If indeed Jesus died in 29 or 30 C.E., and the earliest Gospel was written about 70, then we can understand that the Gospels provide the end results of interpretations about who and what Jesus was, rather than either eye-witness accounts or the results of archival research. But it is the interpretive aspect of the Gospels that abides in Christian awareness, and not the external facts of dates and of authorship.

What does such interpretation amount to? The answer is that while in ordinary Jewish thought of that time it was believed that the coming of the Messiah was destined for the remote future, in the case of Jesus the view was that the Messiah had already come. The great judgment day, believed by Jews as slated for the distant future, was, in the eyes of Jesus and his followers, extremely near at hand. Indeed, the view existed that to the history of God's dealing with his people, beginning with Abraham, there was now being added in Jesus the last and climactic chapter.

Jesus died on the cross. His followers included those who were certain that he was miraculously resurrected, this in advance of the general resurrection. After his resurrection, he ascended to heaven, there to await the near-at-hand moment when he would return (in his "second coming," something still awaited by many Christians) to usher in the great judgment. (In Jewish thought, the Messiah's coming is awaited as a single event in the future; in Christian thought there are two events, the initial coming of the Messiah, which has already taken place, and the future second coming.) The Jewish contrast between "this age" and the "age to come" appears also in Christian thought, in that the first coming of Jesus is regarded as having ushered in the new age, with the fullness of its blessings to emerge at his second coming.

The Gospels, though each of the four has its individuality, give a portrait of Jesus along the following lines: at a time when a certain John the Baptist was calling the people to repentance, and baptizing them in the Jordan River, Jesus too was baptized by him. John, however, was not greater than Jesus, but rather the forerunner, just as Elijah was to be the forerunner of the Messiah. At Jesus' baptism, the heavens opened and a divine voice proclaimed the uniqueness of Jesus as the Son of God. Jesus was then tempted in the Wilderness by Satan, but he successfully resisted Satan. He returned to Galilee. There he began to gather followers and to work cures of the sick and of people possessed by demons. He assured some whom he cured that their sins were forgiven.

These miraculous deeds brought him into conflict with scribes ("scripture teachers") and Pharisees, for it was clear to the people who were in contact with Jesus that he did not teach as they taught but rather with a heightened, unique authority. On the one hand, he gathered more disciples and effected more cures; on the other hand, his conflicts with scribes and Pharisees increased in bitterness, so that the latter determined to have him killed. The controversies centered on aspects of the laws of the written Torah, such as Sabbath observance, and of the oral Torah, such as the washing of the hands. The conflicts grew in extent and bitterness, for Jesus was openly critical, alleging that his opponents were not sincere, but only hypocritical in their observances, and lacking in perspective about what was important and what was trivial. In the synagogue in his home town, Nazareth, he was rejected by his people. He sent out his disciples, with authority over unclean spirits, to preach repentance and to heal the sick. Even the ruler of Galilee, Herod Antipas, wondered who he was for he seemed mysterious. On the return of the disciples he fed five thousand people miraculously, out of five loaves of bread and two fish. When his disciples were crossing the lake of Galilee in a boat, Jesus astounded them by walking on the water.

There ensued more conflicts with Pharisees and Sadducees, and more cures, both in Galilee and in neighboring areas. He fed four thousand people out of seven loaves of bread and a few fish, and there was food left over.

At a place called Caesarea Philippi, he asked his disciples who men thought he was, and who they thought he was. Peter said, "You are the Christ." Jesus then taught the disciples that he was destined to suffer many things, to be rejected by the elders, chief priests, and scribes, and that he would be killed, but that he would rise again after three days. When Peter rebuked him for this destiny, he in turn rebuked Peter. He then told his disciples what they must do if they were truly to follow him. He assured them that even in the lifetime of some of them, they would see the kingdom of God come with power.

He went to a high mountain with three disciples. There he was transfigured (changed in outer form), his garments glistening and white. There on the mountain, Elijah and Moses appeared as though talking to Jesus. A cloud overshadowed them and a voice said, "This is my beloved son; listen to him." Then they no longer saw anyone with them except Jesus. As they came down the mountain, Jesus bade them to tell no one what they had seen, until he had risen from the dead. He assured them that Elijah, who must come first, had already come.

He healed an epileptic boy. Passing through Galilee, he again told his disciples that he would be delivered into the hands of men, be killed, and after three days would rise again. They did not understand him. When the disciples disputed as to which of them was the greatest, he replied that whoever wanted to be first had to be the servant of all. He picked up a child, saying, "Whoever receives one such child in my name receives me, and he who receives me receives him who sent me." He spoke further on what the obligations of his disciples would be.

He began to journey to Jerusalem. When a Pharisee questioned him about divorce, he replied that though Moses had permitted it, this was only because of the hardness of the heart of people. He prohibited divorce.

Approached by a rich young man, faithful to all the commandments, who wanted counsel on how to inherit eternal life, Jesus told him that he must sell all he had and give the money to the poor, for he would then have treasure in heaven. When the countenance of the young man fell, Jesus said, "How hard it will be for those with riches to enter the kingdom of heaven."

Again Jesus informed his disciples of what lay ahead, that is, he would be condemned to death, and that Gentiles would mock and spit on him, scourge him and then kill him, but after three days he would rise from the dead.

Two brothers asked for privileged places when Jesus would return in glory. He denied their request. When the other disciples became indignant at the brothers, Jesus said, "Whoever would be first among you must be your servant, the slave of all." He had come not to be served, but to serve, and to give his life as a ransom for many.

At Jericho, Jesus cured a blind man. Approaching Jerusalem, he sent two disciples to find a colt, which had not been ridden on, and to bring it to him to ride into Jerusalem. The disciples spread garments on the colt and Jesus sat on it. Many spread their garments on the road, and others spread leafy branches. Disciples both in front and behind him shouted, "Hosanna! Blessed be he who comes in the name of the Lord. Blessed be the kingdom of our father David that is coming." Thus he entered Jerusalem. He went into the Temple, but, since it was late, he went to nearby Bethany with his twelve disciples.

The next day he cursed a fig tree. He went into the Temple and drove out the merchants and turned over the seats of the money-changers, saying, "Is it not written, 'My house shall be called a house of prayer for all the nations?' But you have made it a den of robbers." The chief priests and scribes, hearing him, sought a way to destroy him, fearing him be. cause all the populace was astonished at his teaching. The next day, they saw that the fig tree had withered. Jesus said that faith in God could move even mountains. If one believed that he would receive what he prayed for, he would indeed receive it.

In the Temple, chief priests, scribes, and elders demanded to know by what authority Jesus was acting. He refused to tell them. But he told them a parable about wicked tenants of a landlord who went into a foreign community. The landlord sent a series of servants to collect the fruit due him, but the tenants beat some and killed others. The landlord then sent his own son, but the tenants killed him, too. Therefore the landlord would come out and destroy the tenants and give the vineyard to others. The opponents wanted to arrest Jesus, perceiving that he had told the parable against them, but they feared the crowd.

Some Pharisees and Herodians tried to entrap him by asking if it were lawful to pay taxes to Caesar. His reply was, "Give to Caesar the things that are Caesar's and to God the things that are God's." Sadducees, who deny resurrection, sought to trap him by this question: If a woman married a succession of seven brothers, these having died one by one, at resurrection time to which of the seven would she belong? Jesus replied that in the resurrection age there is no marrying, for the resurrected are like angels in heaven. A scribe asked him what was the first of all the commandments. Jesus gave his answer: "Hear, O Israel, the Lord our God, the Lord is one." And he added a second commandment, "You shall love your neighbor as yourself." After this, no one dared ask him any question. Jesus spoke further to condemn the hypocrisy of the scribes.

He predicted that the Temple would be destroyed some day. First, though, would come wars, earthquakes, and famines. In that time his disciples would experience suffering and persecution in synagogues. Brother would rise against brother, and parents and children against each other. The climax of the evil would be the setting up of a desolating sacrilege where it ought not be. False Christs and false prophets would arise. After these disorders, the sun would be darkened, the moon give no light, and stars fall from heaven. Then people would see the Son of man (that is, Jesus) coming in the clouds, with great power and glory, sending out his angels to gather his chosen ones from the ends of the earth. All these events would take place within that generation, but no one but God knew the exact day and hour. The disciples must therefore constantly be on watch for the unknown time which was sure to come.

The time was just before Passover. One of the disciples, Judas Iscariot, to betray Jesus went to the chief priests who promised him money (other accounts say they gave him thirty pieces of silver) for betraying his master. Jesus prepared to observe the Passover, for which there was to be a large upper room ready. When Jesus and the Twelve were at table eating, Jesus announced that one of them would betray him. While they were eating, he took bread, blessed it, and broke it, and said, "Take eat, this is my body." He took a cup of wine from which they all drank, saying, "This is my blood of the covenant which is poured out for you."

After singing a hymn, they went out to the Mount of Olives. There Jesus predicted that they would all desert him, but afterwards he would be raised from the dead, and he would go before them to Galilee. When Peter protested and said that he would not desert him, Jesus said, "You will deny me tonight three times before the cock crows." They moved to Gethsemane where Jesus prayed for his cup (that is, what he was about to experience) to be removed. But he was prepared to accept what God willed, not what he willed. The three disciples with him fell asleep three times as he prayed.

Then Judas came with a crowd, sent by the leaders, carrying clubs and swords. By a kiss Judas identified and betrayed Jesus. The crowd seized him. The disciples forsook him and fled.

The crowd led Jesus to the high priest's, where the chief priests, elders, and scribes were assembled. Peter followed from a distance, entering the courtyard of the high priest, warming himself at the fire. Once assembled, the priests and the Sanhedrin sought testimony by which to condemn Jesus to death, but found none. False witnesses spoke, but their testimony did not agree. The high priest asked him, "Are you the Christ, the Son of the blessed?" He replied, "I am. And you will see the Son of man seated at the right hand of power (God), and coming with the clouds of heaven." The high priest proclaimed these words to be blasphemy. The Sanhedrin condemned him to death, and some spat on him and struck him. The guards received him with blows. Peter, in the meantime, three times before the cock crowed denied having any connection with Jesus.

Jesus was led to Pontius Pilate. Jesus gave little in the way of answers to Pilate. It was Pilate's custom to release one prisoner at the Passover festival. There was among those in prison a man, Barabbas, who had committed murder in "an insurrection." While Pilate offered to release Jesus, the chief priests stirred up the crowd to ask for the release of Barabbas. When Pilate asked, "What shall I do with the man you call the King of the Jews?" they cried again and again, "Crucify him."

Pilate had Jesus scourged and turned over to his soldiers. The soldiers mocked him, dressing him in a purple cloak and putting a crown of thorns on him. They struck him, and spat on him, and mockingly knelt in homage to him. They led him out to crucify him. They compelled a passer-by, Simon of Cyrene, to carry the cross to a place called Golgatha. They offered Jesus wine mixed with myrrh, but he declined it. They then crucified him, dividing his garments among them by lot. With him were crucified two robbers. The inscription of the charge against him read, "The King of the Jews." Passers-by derided him; chief priests spoke to each other, mocking him. The two robbers reviled him.

At the sixth hour (noon), a darkness, lasting three hours, enveloped the land. At the ninth hour, Jesus called in agony, asking only if God had forsaken him. He breathed his last.

A Roman centurion (we would say, sergeant) said, "Truly this man is the Son of God." Women who had followed him in Galilee ministered to him.

A man named Joseph of Arimathea asked Pilate for Jesus' body. Joseph wrapped Jesus in a linen shroud and buried him in a tomb hewn out of a rock and rolled a stone against the door of the tomb, with two women (Mary Magdalene and Mary, mother of Joses), noting where Jesus was laid. On Sunday the two Marys, and one Salome, having bought spices to anoint him, went to the tomb after daybreak, wondering who would roll the stone away. Arriving, they found the stone already rolled back. When they entered the tomb, they saw a young man there dressed in white. He said, "You seek Jesus of Nazareth who was crucified. He has risen and is not here; see the place where they laid him. Now go and tell his disciples and Peter that he is going before you to Galilee. There you will see him, as he told you." The women fled the tomb in great fear.

The above is condensed from the Gospel of Mark. The longer Gospels, particularly Matthew and Luke, differ from Mark by adding to the presentation of the above material a broad array of passages which depict the precise teachings of Jesus. The teachings are found in Matthew in blocks of material, best known in the Sermon on the Mount; in Luke, the teachings of Jesus are found scattered, not presented in blocks. Mark tells nothing of the birth of Jesus; Matthew and Luke, each in their own way, testify to Jesus' miraculous birth, in that he was conceived by his mother Mary as a virgin.

John has a structure quite different from the other three Gospels. In place of a birth narrative, John has a hymn which tells that the divine Word came to earth and took on flesh, thereby becoming the man Jesus. Since John relates fewer incidents than the other Gospels, this Gospel provides something they lack, namely, long soliloquies by Jesus on the significance of events and of beliefs.

We cannot here be concerned with the problems raised by Christian scholars about the Gospels, their differences, and contradictions. An immense body of scholarship deals with these topics, and with the very crucial topic as to how accurate and factual the Gospels are. (I discuss facets of this latter in Chapter 5 on Anti-Semitism.) Here we must try to distill what a Jew should know about the ordinary Christian's approach to the figure of Jesus.

First and foremost is the circumstance that although there are Christians who either doubt this or that detail (such as the virgin birth or the resurrection) or else so reinterpret this or that item (such as the exorcism of demons), such incredulity or reinterpretation on their part does not diminish the figure of Jesus for them in any way. If some Christians are prepared to deny the divinity of Jesus as the Gospels portray it, such Christians nevertheless continue to affirm it, as if the Gospel presentations are of no consequence. For these Christians Jesus remains "our Lord and Master," no matter what difficulties may be conceded to lie in the Gospel accounts. If some Christians deny the virgin birth in its literal sense, they proceed to say that the virgin birth motif is simply a way of trying to describe the eminence of Jesus, and that this unique eminence is not diminished by denying the virgin birth.

If to Jews there are traditions about Jesus that seem incredible, then they need to reckon, first, with comparably incredible traditions (such as God dictating laws to Moses on Sinai), and second, to recognize how thoroughly appealing the central idea in Christianity is, whether it is credible or not. Whereas Judaism speaks of God revealing laws, Christianity teaches that the God of Israel became revealed to men by himself becoming a man. That man, as a babe, was born (so Luke narrates) in a manger. That babe was cherished by his virgin mother, held by some to have been herself free of any

contamination by "original sin." The abundance of portraits
of the Madonna and the child tug at the heartstrings of Christians. It is easy for them to identify with Jesus, for in his
conflicts with fellow Jews, he is presented as always searching
for, and finding, what is authentic in religion. In his conflicts
with Jewish leaders, he is the sturdy man of conviction up
against the inhuman, arrogant, hypocritical, and even deceit-
ful leaders. He is the man of purity, wronged by impure men.
He suffered physical and mental agonies, betrayal, and humil-
iation, all in a thoroughly manly way. And what he went
through, he went through on behalf even of those who
wronged him. Such a career was surely not one of defeat, but
rather of triumph, as attested to by his resurrection.

In short, to a Christian the figure of Jesus is one of an
appeal surpassing that of any other figure in all history.

Since it is a matter of record that Christians have included
those who on their own have ceased to believe that this or
that item is true, it is readily conceivable that a Christian,
spurred by a Jewish spouse, can cease to believe this or that
item, or aggregates of them. Is it as readily conceivable that a
Christian can completely disengage himself or herself from
the perceptions of Jesus which have been his or her property
for many years, or even decades?

But there are further difficulties. Just as it is a Jewish
conviction that Judaism is the greatest of all religions, it is
the Christian conviction that it surpasses Judaism. Do not the
Gospels portray Jesus perceptively discovering the flaws in
Jews and their Judaism?

And what about the contribution of Paul of Tarsus—the
Greek Jew who never knew the human Jesus but who as the
"great apostle" became the second figure in early Christianity
half a generation after Jesus' death? More writings in the New
Testament come from his hand than from any other. Some
indeed think that he, not Jesus, was the true founder of
Christianity (a view I do not share) in that he substituted for
the religion *of* Jesus a religion *about* Jesus (a view I do share).
Did not Paul teach the undeniable truth that Judaism, in

giving primacy to the inherited Jewish laws, was in effect encouraging men to rely on themselves instead of on God? It was because of the basic error in Judaism that Paul had taught that not only could one not achieve salvation by observing the laws, but that the laws were a veritable impediment to salvation, and, indeed, an impetus to the very sins the laws were intended to avert. That is why Paul had declared the laws in the Torah were now abrogated. Because that view about the laws came to dominate in subsequent Christianity, Christians, despite their loyalty to the Bible, feel under no obligation to observe its laws, or its sacred calendar, that is, the array of holy days and festivals enjoined in the Five Books of Moses, and they see no virtue in, or need to, observe Jewish food laws. (For Jews the Laws of Moses have never been abrogated. The Five Books of Moses, written by hand on a parchment scroll, is called the Torah. The high point in the worship service of the synagogue, Orthodox, Conservative, or Reform, occurs when the Torah is ceremoniously taken from its receptacle, the "Holy Ark," and a portion of it read and expounded. The Torah is the Jewish symbol *par excellence*, with an emotional equivalence to Jews that the cross or the crucifix has for Christians.)

What Paul says about the Laws of Moses could not be more uncongenial to Jews. But quite beyond the specific deficits that Paul feels residing in the Law, it is his view that Christianity—Paul never uses this word—is a higher form of religion than the Judaism he was raised in. Accordingly, it is common that Christianity is viewed by Christians as a progression beyond the outmoded Judaism.

Indeed there were early Christians who said that with Christianity on the scene, there was no longer any need for Judaism.

The supposition that a particular religious tradition is intrinsically more valuable and admirable than another leads naturally to the view that the people representative of the better or best are themselves better than other people. Both Christians and Jews have had such suppositions.

Only the rare among Jews understand the distinctions within Christendom, for example, between Roman Catholicism and Protestantism. Indeed, were it not for the violence in recent years in Northern Ireland, most Jews would not even be aware of any distinction at all.

Roman Catholicism emerged, so one may say, around the period about 200-250 C.E.; other dates, both earlier and later, reflect particular definitions, and the dates I here give have only this significance, that Christendom had spread far and wide in the far-flung Roman Empire in the first and second Christian centuries, and only after such spreading did that form of organization eventuate which can be called the Roman Catholic Church. Not all the local enclaves of Christianity entered into the unity that came to enter in Rome; some in remote areas have remained outside to this day. A difference of language affected the unity, especially in that in the eastern parts of Eupore and in Asia Minor, Greek was the language of Christian Scripture and prayer, while in the west Latin arose to supplant the Greek. Persecutions by Roman authorities impeded but did not halt the growth and spread of Christianity, eastward beyond Palestine and as far west as Britain. In Rome after a welter of inner disorders and civil war there came to the throne in 312 the emperor Constantine who overcame his rivals and reestablished the unity of the Empire which had earlier been broken. He built a capital city, Constantinople (which is also called Byzantium and Istanbul). A predecessor, Diocletian, had tried by persecution to crush Christianity. Constantine, in sharp reversal, made Christianity the official religion of the Roman Empire in 325. A half century after Constantine's death, the Roman Empire split into the eastern kingdom centered in Constantinople (the Byzantine) and the western centered in Rome. Out of differences of political rule and language there emerged the rival Christian entities, the Eastern and the Roman churches.

The emperor Constantine in 325 convened an assembly of bishops for a "council" meeting held in Nicea in what is today Turkey; it was the first of many subsequent councils.

Often Christian history is divided into chronological segments, with the Council of Nicea interpreted by some as the end of the first segment, which thus runs from Jesus to 325; others speak of the age immediately after Jesus as the "apostolic age," and a second age from about 50 to 325. A name for the age before Nicea is often "patristic," that is, the age of the fathers.

During the patristic age organization, liturgy, church government, and officials emerged into forms which persist to our day. Since Rome prior to Constantine was the capital, it became natural for the Bishop of Rome to be regarded unofficially as the head of the church, the Pope. In the course of time, this recognition went beyond the unofficial, and the pope emerged as the ruler of the western, Latin church; his authority was not recognized in the eastern Greek church, which was headed by the Patriarch of Constantinople. The structure of the church in the west, with gradations of the clergy, was to lead to offices such as cardinal, archbishop, bishop, priest, deacon (and other minor offices, most of which have disappeared). The liturgy became more or less fixed.

After the Council of Nicea, there was ordinarily a union of church and state in the west. At Nicea a certain heresy had been denounced, and the power of the state was available to stamp out this heresy by force. It is possible after Nicea to speak of an official distinction between orthodoxy (right doctrine) and heresy (wrong doctrine).

There arose a group of seven so-called sacraments, ceremonial acts, which imply some supernatural aspect over and beyond the purely human act itself. Two of the seven (baptism and the ceremony of eating bread and drinking wine; this latter is known by different names, such as Lord's Supper, the Holy Mass, or the Eucharist) are attributed in origin in the New Testament to Jesus; the other five include confirmation, marriage, penance, holy orders, and unction. Even this array of sacraments is in a sense analogous to the full array of laws as observed by Judaism, with the difference that, in Judaism, the array of laws is greatly more numerous, and conventionally counted as 613 (for which there is the Hebrew way of saying 613, namely *taryag*). However, rites in Judaism are not sacraments in the sense of in themselves containing a supernatural element or effect; also, in Judaism the communicant himself performs them, rather than having them performed for, with, or to him by a priest as in Catholicism.

The necessary participation of a priest in the sacraments supposes that he has proper credentials. The Christian theory is that a person who has gone through the sacrament of holy orders receives authority from the person who presided at the rite, and that person in turn had himself received such authority from the one presiding at his own rite. Hence, an unbroken chain of authority exists that goes back to Jesus himself. The usual name for this theory of an unbroken transmitted authority going back to Jesus is called "apostolic succession."

That is to say, the church developed into a complex organization, with clearly designated officials, recorded regulations (canon law) for the governing of the church and its communicants, a clear sense of the distinction between orthodoxy and heresy, a growing body of writings, including the work of men eminent in scholarship and in philosophy. It was thus prepared for the unique role it achieved in what we might call the "Middle Ages," that vague period from the fifth to the sixteenth century. By the end of the fifth century, the pagan religions had been superseded completely, and the pagan heritage of philosophical schools ended. This pagan legacy (the Greek and Roman philosophers and writers) was preserved and even copied in the monasteries that arose. The phrase "dark ages" (offensive to some Christians) is an exaggerated way of describing the transition of the classical learning of the Greeks and that of the Romans from living schools and academies into the dormant libraries of the monasteries.

The Middle Ages are correctly spoken of as the age of a

Christian civilization. Two main developments characterize this civilization. First, the Roman Catholic Church attained great power, with the pope having the authority to confirm, or even designate, the political ruler, as was repeatedly the case in connection with the so-called Holy Roman Empire. The papacy won out in some repeated conflicts with regional rulers over the question of whether the pope or the regional ruler had authority over the clergy in his region, especially over who had the right to appoint bishops. A negative consequence was the all-too-frequent involvement of the papacy in international power politics, with the result that kings vied with each other for favor with the pope, and the papacy became a prize for adventurers. At times there were two rival claimants of the office of pope, and occasionally at times three. For the period from 1309 to 1377, the succession of popes which later came to be regarded as legitimate ruled the church not from Rome but from Avignon, France, for Rome had become unsafe.

Second, the church influenced or even dominated all facets of life. The sacraments, symbolized by baptism in early infancy and extreme unction at death, covered the full span of an individual's life. Weekly the communicant made his penitential penance (confession) before his local priest, who then absolved him of sin.

A high office, such as bishop, was one of power. It could become one of wealth. Highly placed clerics were able to build sumptuous palaces. As wealth and power increased, cathedrals of immense size and beauty were erected. They were enhanced through the work of sculptors and painters, and the divine worship beautified by musical performers and, later, by new works written by gifted composers. Art and music were Christian art and Christian music. The study of the ancient Greek and Roman classics was revived (the revival is called the Renaissance). Great minds fashioned blends of Greek philosophy and Christian doctrine, and universities were founded by churchmen. The civilization was Christian in that Christianity penetrated all facets of existence, whether that of an impoverished, ignorant peasant or that of a duke or a king of culture and of enough wealth to be a patron of the arts and scholarship.

The geographical extent of Christianity had become reduced when Islam came onto the scene in the seventh century, and took as its own Asia Minor, Palestine, North Africa, and even Spain. Within Europe, the Eastern Orthodox church persisted in its independence from Rome, and the strains between east and west were repeatedly acute. The eastern church and the Islamic conquests were symbols of limits which obstructed the universality of the sway of the papacy at Rome. But even where that sway continued, Catholic Europe consisted of many languages, nations, and many kings. The unity of Catholic Europe was destined to be fragile.

Here and there the power and wealth of upper clergy led to corruption, both in matters of money and of personal morality. Around the seventh century, it had become customary for the clergy of the west to be unmarried, celibate. But celibacy was violated even by cardinals and popes. The power of the clergy led to frequent abuses respecting power, money, and morality. From within the church, the need for reforms was expressed. One effort towards reforms was the creation of orders of priests (later of nuns) who took special vows of poverty, chastity, and obedience and who lived in communal monasteries in a simplicity that was in marked contrast to the luxury of cathedrals and clerical palaces.

Here and there some movement cropped up, restricted in scope and time, entailing some dissent or even some heresy, and the church assumed the power to stamp out the heresy and destroy the heretics. In Spain especially, orthodoxy was raised to such a soaring new height of church demand as to give rise to the Inquisition, an organized inquiry into the true faith of believers. In Spain, after Christian reconquest, in order to escape expulsion, Jews and Moors alike went through a conversion that was only perfunctory, while they secretly retained both their beliefs and practices. The officials of the Inquisition used both honest and dishonest informers to harass the Marranoes (secret Jews) and the Moriscoes (the converting Moors), and by extremes of personal torture elicited purported confessions, with the confessors then burnt to death at the stake.

In England a different type of issue had to be faced. It was that of translating the Bible from Latin into English. The church was opposed to such translation. Why is difficult to say. Possibly the church wished for the knowledge of the Bible to be restricted to its clergy, lest the Bible become a sort of rival in authority to the church. Possibly the church was sensitive to the circumstance that there was a great disparity between the relative bareness of the Christianity of the Gospels, in which there is no mention of pope, or of cardinals, or of cathedrals, and the highly developed Christianity of the times. (Jews should remember that words such as *rabbi* and *synagogue* are similarly absent from the Hebrew Bible, for Synagogue Judaism and Roman Catholicism are both extensive developments *after* their respective biblical periods.) Whatever the explanation, translation from Latin into the vernacular (the language of a particular country) was regarded as prohibited and punishable.

There were, then, the seeds of reform and of strong reaction against the Roman Catholic Church and its officials well before the actual revolt broke into the open in 1517. With that revolt the name of an erstwhile German Catholic priest, Martin Luther (1483-1546) is associated. His revolt focused on a minor matter, the question of "indulgences," a remission of temporal, immediate punishment for sins, a remission granted by the church. Of special importance for people at that time was that such indulgences could also be acquired for one's deceased relatives, thus shortening the duration of their punishment in purgatory. It had become the practice that indulgences be granted for money, that is, sold;

hence, there were those in the church who trafficked in the sale of indulgences. Luther's initial step was his challenge of the authenticity of this traffic.

The factors which led to the outbreak of the revolt were multiple and complex, entailing political and economic currents, language and cultural differences, and responses to persistent abuses despite some earnest but ineffective inner reforms. Perhaps a Jew can best understand the eruption which tore western Christianity into the two divisions, Roman Catholicism and Protestantism, in terms of what was involved in the Reformation, and of what was not involved! In Catholicism, *authority* lies in both Scripture and in the church as the guardian and official teacher of that Scripture. Protestants attribute authority to Scripture alone. The Roman Catholic Church, through its *priests*, regards itself as the intermediary between God and man. Protestantism stresses its *lay* character, believing that man approaches God directly, needing no intermediary. From this standpoint, the entire historical development of a church structure and an elaborate clergy with many ranks was viewed as an aberration.

The Roman Catholic Church has seven sacraments, Protestants usually only two, Baptism and the Eucharist, explicitly mentioned in the New Testament.

Lutheran churches have maintained in their form of worship a rich liturgy which externally is not much changed from the Roman Catholic service or mass, although certain common elements are interpreted differently. But other Protestant churches (except the Episcopal) incline to a modest liturgy, and some to a bare one. Ordinarily the usual Protestant church worship service, apart from introductory, closing, and recessional hymns, consists of two readings from the New Testament, one from the Gospels, and the other from the Epistles. Normally the Lord's Prayer is then said. Some churches include one of the ancient creeds. A collection plate into which worshipers can put gifts of money (the offering) precedes the sermon. The sermon is more important in a Protestant church (as is the case in Reform and Conservative Judaism) than in the Roman or Anglo-Catholic churches, where a worship service without a sermon (as in Orthodox Judaism) is not unusual.

A Catholic worship service centers in the Lord's Supper (also called the High Holy Mass or the Eucharist), in which the communicant eats a piece of broken bread, symbolic of the body of Jesus. At one time there was the accompanying drinking of wine, symbolic of the blood of Jesus, but this now occurs less often in Roman Catholicism. Protestants, however, use both the bread or wafer and the wine. (Prohibitionist churches use grape juices!). Among Protestants the Eucharist (usually called by Protestants Holy Communion) is not celebrated weekly, but only once or twice monthly. Protestants apart from Lutherans and Episcopalians generally regard the ceremony less supernaturally than do Catholics, since they view it as a memorial of Jesus, denying that the wafer and wine, in effect, are transformed into the "real" body and blood of Jesus.

For a Catholic to "take communion," he must be free of mortal sin, by first having made "confession" and having been "absolved" by a priest. Confession in this sense does not exist among Protestants. The minimum obligation on Catholics for confession and communion is once a year. The custom, though, is to go to communion each Sunday, but to confession only as often "mortal sin" recurs. Among Protestants such attendance is advocated, but it is not compulsory. (Among Jews, it is the home that is the chief center of the religious life, with the synagogue a supplement; synagogue attendance is not obligatory on the part of Jews, but certain prayers, such as prayers for the deceased on the anniversary of the date of the death, are supposed to be recited in the synagogue, and thus indirectly obligatory attendance can be inferred for such occasions.)

Protestantism became subdivided in a great many ways; by geography into ethnic, national, and linguistic groups; by dissent and withdrawal from official or dominant churches by some entities which remained small and by some which grew; by differences in restricted aspects of doctrine, or differences in the emphasis put on certain doctrines; or through a development in which a group within a dominant church took on some special character, and then eventually became separate from that church. Some examples may clarify, especially since the examples chosen should help to illuminate the special uniqueness of Protestantism in contrast to Roman Catholicism. Thus, mention was made of infant baptism in the Catholic church. Since obviously a baby scarcely chooses to be baptized, and, in not choosing, abstains from exercizing the will to be baptized, there arose among Protestants those who denied the validity of infant baptism. Demanding that baptized people be baptized again by choice at maturity, they became known as anabaptists (*ana* is a Greek prefix meaning "again"). In time infant baptism ceased among such people, and the "again" was dropped, yielding the name "Baptist."

A French scholar and leader, John Calvin, who settled in Geneva, serves as another example. He stressed the theme (found in the Epistles of Paul and in the teachings of the fifth-century personality, Augustine) that God saves sinners by grace, and not because of any merit at all on the part of sinners for their good deeds. Man is unable, indeed, to do anything of merit, for by his very nature he is unworthy and depraved. Whom, then, does God save? Those whom he has predestined (that is, divinely decided in advance) for salvation. The accentuation of these themes by Calvin appealed to various groups and persons; principal among the followers of Calvin was John Knox who in Scotland founded a "Calvinist" church, governed by *presbyters* (elders), thus establishing the Presbyterian Church, which there for the most part supplanted the Roman Catholic Church, in Scotland.

Another example is the Methodist Church. It was founded by a priest of the Church of England, John Wesley, and was within that church. The systematic manner of their observances led to the name, at first derisive, of "Methodists." When the Methodists wished to have the right to appoint bishops, conflict arose that led to the separation of Methodists from the Church of England. The Methodist Church, transplanted to the United States, has grown in numbers and significance.

It is not possible here to trace all the various shadings within Protestantism, such as the founding of new sects on issues as to whether baptism is to be by sprinkling or by immersion, and if by immersion, whether in a stream of running water or in a stagnant pool or lake. Nor is it possible to do more than mention that some Protestant churches have bishops (e.g., Methodists) with authority over ministers and/ or churches, whereas in general Protestant churches have local congregational autonomy. Some churches have bodies of rules, some do not. Yet the general principle is the inviolability of the individual conscience, and the view that neither the state nor an organized church can usurp the freedom of the individual conscience. In America, by and large, national Protestant church organizations derive whatever authority they may have over a local church (if any!) only from the voluntary consent of the governed local churches.

Protestant bodies also have had characteristic inner tensions and strains of their own and, in the case of some American denominations these strains have resulted in division and bad feeling. On the premise that salvation lies in Scripture, as the free conscience interprets it, how does one understand Scripture? The rise of biblical scholarship, essentially in the eighteenth century but flowering in the nineteenth, led to division concerning the religious legitimacy of that scholarship, for basic questions were brought into the open because of it. Is the Bible divine and free of error? Or was there some human factor, small or even large, in the writing of the biblical books? Did Moses indeed write the Five Books of Moses, at God's dictation, or did these books grow by accretion over the centuries, a growth discernible in four documents: J (dated 850-750); E (750-650); D (621); and P (about 400). Did the Five Books of Moses, in fact, reach their present form long after Moses' time? Was

Matthew, as church tradition held, the earliest of the Gospels, originally written in Hebrew, and was Mark a later abridgement of it? Or was Mark the earliest Gospel, composed in Greek, and a source utilized by the author of Matthew who wrote in Greek, not in Hebrew? Was it admissible to depart from the views inherited from the ancient past about the sacred writings?

Moreover, must one take literally biblical accounts of events (such as creation in six days, the splitting of the Red Sea, or the virgin birth, or Jesus' walking on the water)? Could these events be viewed either as symbols, or else as relics of a primitive supernaturalism, but without literal belief incumbent on the communicant? Is the history found in Scripture, even where no supernatural miracles are related, reliable and fully accurate, or is it not? Scarcely any Protestant communion escaped being touched by the rise of contradictory viewpoints, with many scholars freely discarding traditional views, and others insisting that no deviation was tolerable. Some communions were split in two, as between modernists and fundamentalists. Roman Catholics and Jews, though touched by such disputes, were in a sense much less affected, simply because the Bible is less central to them than it is to Protestants.

There are some two hundred fifty national bodies of Protestants in the United States. Most of them fit into the broad categories of Episcopalian, Presbyterian, Baptist, Lutheran, Congregationalist, or German "pietistic" sects. Two bodies are American in origin, the Church of Jesus Christ of the Latter-Day Saints and the Church of Christ, Scientist (Christian Science). A frontier union of members of diverse churches led to the formation of a new entity, the Disciples of Christ, later known as the Christian Church. In general, the greater the measure there is of a set liturgy in a Protestant church, the more that church was spared the extremes of the modernist-fundamentalist schisms. The less liturgical it was, the more prone to such division it was. The Civil War added another facet of geographical division as between loyalty to the Union or to the Confederacy.

Accordingly, when one speaks of Protestantism, it is less to the point to speak of the historic churches I have mentioned than to speak of modernism, liberal conservatism, or fundamentalism. The denominational divisions abide, but what really divides Protestants is the issue summarized in the words *nonfundamentalist* and *fundamentalist*. By a fundamentalist one means a Protestant who believes that the Bible is literally divine in origin, that it is free of all error, and that it is the one true guide for living. The radical modernist goes to the other extreme, viewing the Bible as essentially human, as a product of the ancient age that produced it, true in spirit or intent rather than free from error; it is one general source of inspiration among many others rather than the specific guide for living. The liberal conservative is somewhere between the two, and is liberal in the sense of feeling freer to choose to depart from tradition than does the fundamentalist, but he is generally more retentive of traditionalism than is the radical modernist.

What a Jew would encounter in marrying a Protestant, whether a modernist or fundamentalist, is an orientation to the Bible very much different from his own. This is so because for a Jew the Bible is viewed through the prism of the centuries of accumulated Jewish thought and interpretation. A fundamentalist Protestant would frequently "prove" a contention simply by quoting a verse (and often, too, by quoting the name of the biblical book, and the chapter and verse). Much of Jewish religious practice being in *origin* rabbinic rather than biblical, Jews are not accustomed to quote the Bible, and when they chance to do so, they would assume that there is some traditional interpretation of that verse that has a priority over some personal view. Jews moreover would not place great reliance on any translation, even one made by Jews, but ascribe genuine authority only to the Hebrew Bible. A fundamentalist quotes Scripture more frequently than nonfundamentalists (and probably is exceedingly more familiar with it).

A Protestant clergyman (except for Episcopalians) is not a priest, and not an intermediary between his parishioners and

God. In this regard he is like a rabbi; neither a Protestant minister nor a rabbi is deemed to be of a higher religious rank than any one else. Indeed it is a Protestant principle that to be a farmer, or a carpenter, or a physician, or a religious functionary reflects no gradation in religious rank, since God calls all men for a vast variety of pursuits, and the pursuits of men are the results of God's call to them. A Protestant minister steps out of his role if he presumes to direct a parishioner to some obligation, for the conscience of the parishioner must not be violated even by his minister. A parishioner will look to his minister for counsel and guidance, to the end that he or she can make a decision in full and clear conscience. A rabbi would inform an inquiring congregant what the relevant Jewish attitude involved in a decision would be, and expect the congregant to abide by the conveyed Jewish attitude; obedience is, of course, implied in such a Jewish situation but it is obedience to the Jewish tradition and not to the person of the rabbi. The rabbi is essentially a resource person qualified by the fullness and exactness of his knowledge; his knowledge implies authority, his person none.

In Roman Catholicism and in the Eastern Orthodox Church, on the other hand, the priest can reasonably expect obedience to him as a person, and the parishioner is reared to obey the priest. In very recent years, there has been great upheaval in the Roman Catholic Church, what with priests and nuns leaving their religious posts to marry. While there are Roman Catholics who today dare to disobey the priest, this act of daring is totally out of keeping with the historic Catholic way, which is the way of obedience.

Among the radical modernists (such as Unitarians) there are some who are not accustomed invariably to end a prayer with a phrase such as, "we ask this in the name of our Lord Jesus Christ." For most Protestant and Catholic clergyman the use of this formula or a kindred phrase is as natural as breathing, and for them to abstain from using it unnatural. Since Jesus is not regarded by a Jew as his Lord, one can

understand that a Jew would not regard a prayer so ending as
representing him, even though he might share without reservation in the words and meaning of the prayer up to the last
phrase. I *think* (but am not sure) that many American Jews
have been attuned to this sort of thing, through hearing
Christian invocations and benedictions over the radio or television, and take little notice of it. Yet it happens from time
to time that a Christian clergyman, participating in a
synagogue function (such as a vestry room meeting of the
National Conference of Christians and Jews), uses the phrase
and discovers, to his surprise and horror, that he has thereby
offended Jews! I know of one incident where one Christian
minister rebuked another for doing this sort of thing; the
rebuked minister was in turn offended, for he found it hard
to understand why his normal way of prayer to God should,
of all things, be offensive to anybody.

It is necessary to say frankly that a great number of Jews,
recalling persecution in the name of Jesus, consider it
inappropriate or even worse merely to pronounce his name.
There have been Jews who have written me to berate me, not
for what I have written about Jesus, but for having written
about him at all. I believe that I understand the depth of this
kind of Jewish response, since my own parents came to the
United States after pogroms which began with the ringing of
church bells, and I think my mother never heard church bells
without shivering.

If it is true, as I think it is, that I am a reasonably objective
student of Christianity, especially earliest Christianity, then it
is also true that I can speak about Jesus, neither sharing in
Christian convictions about him nor in the limited and negative response found among some Jews. But it is a fact that
such a negative syndrome about Jesus exists among some
Jews. I think that most Jews, though lacking Christian convictions, do have a healthy curiosity about Jesus. But I must
not conceal the reality that to some Jews the word *Jesus*
epitomizes the dismay which has accumulated for many Jews
at the indignities and discriminations and persecutions at the

hands of Christians. Some clergy, including rabbis, have wished or demanded an assurance of an intermarrying couple that the children be reared in that clergyman's faith. It needs to be said that often an objection by a Jewish parent to a son's or daughter's marrying a Christian is the thought that one's own grandchild might some day repeat the Christian phrases that are, right or wrong, so painful to the grand-parent. Perhaps this is a bit of reprehensible bigotry on the part of Jews. Or perhaps the past understandably leaves an ineradicable imprint on people. I do not intend to condone what I here describe. I only attempt to describe reality.

Perhaps Jews are able to come to some sympathetic under-standing of Christianity, without sharing in Christian con-victions. Even as Jews do not succeed in understanding the Trinity (as some American Christians do not), yet are ready to accept the assurance that Christianity is a monotheism, devoted to the worship of the God of Israel, I doubt that Jews can or will ever understand sympathetically the celibacy of Catholic priests and nuns. (Indeed some Catholics too question celibacy.) In the Jewish scheme of things, although even few Jews know it, the first law to be encountered in the Book of Genesis is the injunction, "Be fruitful and multiply." There is in main-line Judaism not the slightest suggestion that sex is in any way evil (except when abused) or that reason-able gratification of the other senses, by good food or drink, is wrong in any way at all. Jews, then, seeing no virtue in celibacy, cannot grasp, despite explanation, how a man or a woman can choose to be a priest or a nun, nor appreciate the supposition that such a life has a sublimity to it (How beauti-fully and eloquently I once heard a nun expound this!) beyond any other form of life. It is not that Jews are con-temptuous of celibacy or of those who choose it, but only that Jews can understand Protestantism much more easily than they can Catholicism, for their view of Catholicism is influenced or even shaped by their mystification at clerical celibacy. That Catholics have had dietary laws (such as the now obsolete ban of meat on Friday) and in a sense have "laws" which in a sense Protestants lack, predisposes Jews to view Catholicism as closer to Judaism than Protestantism. Yet celibacy enters in to overbalance things. I think it right There is a wide division between Protestants and Catholics about Mary. That difference might be put in this way, that though some Protestants would join with Catholics in accepting the traditional stance concerning the virgin birth, few Protestants would accept the doctrine of the Immaculate Conception. Protestants do not pray to Mary as Catholics do. I think it right to say that, quite apart from the question of *credibility* of the virgin birth, Jews see nothing admirable in it, and tend to think it a needless doctrine. Similarly, when Jews hear of the Immaculate Conception (Mary being free of the taint of guilt inherited from the disobedience of Adam in the Garden of Eden), they find it exceedingly difficult to grasp.

Catholic children in the past (before Vatican Council II in the mid-sixties) were ordinarily taught proper beliefs out of a manual called a catechism, with the manual ordinarily consisting of questions and answers, the pupil usually memorizing both question and answer. The Rosary is a prayer, divided into units of ten, each preceded by the Lord's Prayer and followed by the prayer, Hail, Mary, found in the Gospel of Luke 1:42. One counts the tens on a chain of beads. The "counting of the Rosary" was once the most usual form of private devotions among Catholics, but seems no longer to be so; it is unknown among Protestants. The recollection from childhood of the catechism and the use of the Rosary are characteristic of older Catholic people, especially women. Younger Catholics are apt to have had a different rearing, the product of reforms stemming from Vatican Council II. The Rosary chain of beads, where it is still used, has ordinarily been blessed by a priest and is therefore all the more precious to a Catholic. Adults have often used their childhood Rosary all their lives.

I have commented repeatedly already that just as there are Jews who are Jews in name only, so too are there nominal Christians, or "lapsed ones." The marital tension between a practicing religious person and a nonpracticing mate of a different background varies and is usually dependent on the attitude of the nonpracticing party. If one party is content to abstain from impinging by word or deed on the other, the situation is quite different from the determination of the practicing one to win or force the mate either into active religious adherence or else into a non- or anti-stance. Sympathetic tolerance is not the same as studied indifference, and studied indifference not the same as amused contempt. When the religious background is diverse, studied indifference is less a threat than amused contempt. If the backgrounds are as diverse as Jewish and Christian, the tensions between someone who practices religion and one who practices none can be acute and can erupt devastatingly.

In our time it is not unusual that an intermarriage occurs between a Jew and a Christian in which both are totally indifferent to his or her religion. In such instances, sociological factors can be the cause of tension and distress but these normally can be met. Perhaps one word of caution might be in order. Where people are genuinely without religion, and have been so at a time well before they have met, the situation is far different from one in which their meeting and desire to marry each other pushes them into their common nonreligion. In a sense, in such a situation, a peculiar kind of conversion is taking place, a conversion to nonreligion, and it is fraught with some of the same dangers and uncertainties of all conversions for convenience, for example, lapses of memory followed by revived sentiments, or by the awakening of latent loyalties. If perhaps groom and bride can forefend against mutual tensions, they ought to know in advance how united they will be if something arises to perplex them. Apparently many people in our time are able to live in the no-man's land of no religion. But for how long? And what happens to people of no religion when a child is born? Is a baby boy to be circumcized or not? And, later, when the child is ready for marriage, will the marriage of a nonreligious child to a religious adherent be welcome? And what happens to a person of no religion at death? Will there be a family plot available in a nonsectarian cemetery or in a Jewish or Christian one? What sort of funeral service or burial will there be?

At the risk of seeming to play with words, the opinion needs to be expressed that nonreligion can be as conducive of partisanship and even bigotry as religion itself. While it is to be conceded that a common nonreligion does not present as great a threat to a marriage as diversity in religion, nonreligion provides its own array of possible problems.

One must ask also whether a life of nonreligion is as rich as a religious life. Surely there is need for constant renewal as the years go on of whatever accord was reached at the time of the wedding.

But can a religious Christian understand a nonreligious Jew, or a religious Jew a nonreligious Christian? Perhaps. I suspect that understanding and basic unity are more elusive here than between two people who acknowledge diverse religions.

5

Anti-Semitism

The word *Semitic* has as its background the scientific study of languages, which recognizes that, first, certain languages are very closely related to one another and constitute a family, and second, that certain other families of languages are totally unrelated. Thus, Greek, Latin, German, and the Indian language Sanskrit, however different they are, are related to each other and probably have a common origin in some now-lost ancestral language; this family has been known by three terms, with roughly the same import: *Indo-European*, or else *Indo-Germanic*, or else *Aryan*. This latter Sanskrit word means "best," "high rank," or "aristocratic."

Quite a different family of languages includes Arabic and Hebrew, which are clearly living languages, and such dead languages as Phoenician and Babylonian. The Bible ascribes the settlement of the area where Babylonia was to Shem, the oldest son of Noah. From Shem is derived the usual name for this other family of language, the Semitic.

The word *anti-Semitism* was born out of nineteenth-century European developments, especially nationalism, and out of a theory that within a nation all its people ought to be of a common stock, of a common "race." The words *Aryan* and *Semite* came to be used as descriptive not of languages but of people, and Jews were classified as Semites, even though the languages they spoke were such Aryan tongues as French or Italian, or, indeed, Yiddish. The choice of the word at that time, *Aryan*, was deliberate; it was a consequence of the conceit that "Aryans" represented people inherently superior to the people of other stocks.

By this time in western Europe, the age-old religious hostility to Jews on the part of Christians had come to an end,

and, indeed, in some nineteenth-century events Christians
rose in defense of Jews.

What had been this Christian hostility?

First, perhaps, it needs to be noted that hostility to Jews
existed in the Graeco-Roman world prior to Christianity.
Why? Because Jews resident in the Graeco-Roman world
were granted the right to live under Jewish laws, and therefore lived a life apart. The Book of Esther puts into the
mouth of the premier Haman these words addressed to the
Persian ruler Ahasuerus: "There is a people scattered and
dispersed in all the [127] provinces of your kingdom whose
laws are different from those of all other people, and who do
not observe the king's laws. It is not advantageous to the king
to tolerate them." While this setting, according to the narrative in the Book of Esther, is ostensibly Persia, there are
modern scholars who believe that the Book of Esther used
Persia in a fictional way to describe a recurrent situation
which existed in the Graeco-Roman world.

Why did Haman speak those words to the king? Because
on Haman's elevation to the highest office "all the king's
servants bowed down and prostrated themselves before
Haman. But the Jew Mordecai would not do so, for Jews
would not bow down to any human, whether a premier, or a
king, or an emperor." When Haman saw that Mordecai would
not bow to him, he was consumed with fury, but, disdaining
to lay hands on Mordecai alone, sought to destroy all the
Jews. In the Graeco-Roman world, it was well known that
Jews would not take part in the worship of the emperor.

Moreover, Jews, in conformity with one of the Ten Commandments, would not worship idols. Since the Jewish God
was conceived of as pure spirit, and lacking all form or physical being, pagans dismissed Jews as atheists! (Prior to the
triumph of Christianity, Christians were regarded by pagans
in exactly the same way as were Jews.)

We know of local conflicts that were exceptions. In 38-39
C.E., the pagans in Alexandria, Egypt wrought a cruel
pogrom (if we may use this Russian word in an anachronistic

way) on their fellow Jews, and the Roman governor Flaccus was most unenergetic in protecting the safety of Jews and in sustaining the rights legally given them. The price of difference where principle is involved can be a high one, and Jews paid that price in Alexandria, both physically and also in encountering hostile, scurrilous writings (similar to some writings later composed by pagans against Christians).

Christian "anti-Semitism"* has a different origin. Christianity was born within Judaism, was separated, and then explained and justified its separateness by contending that it was superior to Judaism, and, indeed, that Christians had replaced Jews as God's own people, and that Jews had been rejected by God for rejecting Jesus, and, indeed, were a damned people.

As Christianity spread to the Roman Empire, Christians found it an embarrassment that Jesus had been put to death by the Romans. So Christians began to contend, with increased forcefulness as time went on, that it was the Jews, not Romans, who were responsible. The Romans did perform the execution, but only after the Jews had held an unfair and illegal trial of Jesus. The Roman official, Pontius Pilate, then the procurator (roughly meaning governor), had sought to free the innocent Jesus, but he had weakly succumbed to the bitter hostility of the crowd of Jews. Accordingly, though the Romans had executed Jesus, it was in reality the Jews who caused his death. Which Jews? In answer, all Jews, of all time and of every place. The New Testament has many passages of this kind. The theme was enlarged and deepened after the New Testament age by some of the church fathers. In perspective we should recall that Jews and Christians wrote in as hostile a way against pagans. Christians often wrote in as hostile a way against each other as they did against Jews. Moreover, in the sixteenth century Protestants and Catholics wrote against each other in an even worse way,

*Let it be recalled that mention has been made of Jewish "persecution" of Christians. The Gospel according to John recurrently alleges that Christians were expelled from the synagogues. There is no reason to doubt this. However, Christians were only one of several dissident groups the judgment on whom was unfavorable.

and they waged wars against each other. Nasty writing is far from unknown in the religious legacy of western man.

What is different in the case of Jews and Christians is that whereas so much of the typical dismal hatred that dots the history of religion is known only to research scholars, the Christian hostility to Jews made its way into writings that became part of the New Testament, and these writings have been perpetuated in the Christian religion, preached on in Christian churches, and taught in church schools.

In our day, classes of Christian children visit synagogue services and classes of Jews visit church services. How is a Jew, visiting a church service, to react to the public reading of this passage?

> "Now when they had passed through Amphipolis and Appolonia, they came to Thessalonica, where there was a synagogue of the Jews. And Paul went in, as was his custom, and for three weeks he argued with them from the scriptures.... And some of them were persuaded, and they joined Paul and Silas; as did a great many of the devout Greeks and not a few of the leading women. But the Jews* were jealous and, taking some wicked fellows of the rabble, they gathered a crowd, set the city in an uproar, and attacked the house of Jason, seeking to bring them out [Paul and Silas] to the people. And when they could not find them, they dragged Jason and some of the brethren before the city authorities, crying, 'These men who have turned the world upside down have come here also, and Jason has received them; and they are all acting against the decrees of Caesar, saying that there is another king, Jesus'.... But when the Jews of Thessalonica later learned that the word of God was being proclaimed by Paul at Beroea, they came there too, stirring up and inciting the crowds."
>
> (Acts 17:1-2, 4-7, 13)

Here is another passage:

> "Jesus then said to the Jews who had believed in him, 'If you continue in my word, you are truly my disciples, and you will know the truth, and the truth will make you free.' They answered him, 'We are descendants of Abraham and have never been in

*Christian friends who have read this book in manuscript tell me that they at no time associated the Jews of this and similar passages, that is, the Jews of ancient times and remote places, with the modern Jews whom they know. Even while regretting that there are such passages, they feel that possibly oversensitivity enters in.

bondage to any one. How is it that you say "You will be made
free"?'

Jesus answered them, 'Truly, truly, I say to you, every one who
commits sin is a slave to sin. The slave does not continue in the
house for ever; the son continues for ever. So if the Son makes
you free, you will be free indeed. I know that you are descendants
of Abraham; yet you seek to kill me, because my word finds no
place in you. I speak of what I have seen with my Father, and you
do what you have heard from your father.'

They answered him, 'Abraham is our father.' Jesus said to them,
'If you were Abraham's children, you would do what Abraham
did, but now you seek to kill me, a man who has told you the
truth which I heard from God; this is not what Abraham did. You
do what your father did.' They said to him, 'We were not born of
fornication; we have one Father, even God.' Jesus said to them, 'If
God were your Father, you would love me, for I proceeded and
came forth from God; I came not of my own accord, but he sent
me. Why do you not understand what I say? It is because you
cannot bear to hear my word. You are of your father the devil,
and your will is to do your father's desires. He was a murderer
from the beginning, and has nothing to do with the truth, because
there is no truth in him. When he lies, he speaks according to his
own nature, for he is a liar and the father of lies. But, because I
tell the truth, you do not believe me. Which of you convicts me of
sin? If I tell the truth, why do you not believe me? He who is of
God hears the words of God; the reason why you do not hear
them is that you are not of God.' "

(John 8:31-47)

Many other passages of comparable vein occur in the New
Testament, and therefore have been and are read and taught
in Christian churches. When Christianity became the official
religion of the Roman Empire, a successive aggregate of laws
translated this theological hostility into legal limitations on
and discriminations against Jews. Major persecutions of Jews
by Christians were at times mob actions, spurred by irrespon-
sible fanatics, but at other times they were spurred by
responsible local church officials. Those legal disabilities
which were removed as modern democracies emerged, were
Christian in origin. The medieval law requiring the wearing of
a "Jew badge" was Christian; the creation of the physical
ghetto was Christian. In fairness, it needs to be said that

while Christian laws limited the freedoms of Jews, it was consistently the practice of high church officials sturdily to protect Jews in the limited freedoms they were allowed.

One can speculate how it was that Jews survived in Christian Europe at all. Granted their economic usefulness, if only on a temporary basis, the first answer lies in the very ethics of Christian doctrine which exercised some restraint on cruelty. Moreover, in perspective, the cruelties in the Middle Ages were part of the mores of the time and were widely practiced by Christians on each other; for example, in the First Crusade in 1096, the Crusaders wrought havoc on the Jews in the Rhineland, but in the Fourth Crusade (1202-1204) the western Christians sacked Christian Constantinople.

But a further answer is of great importance, for while Christian "anti-Semitism" made racial anti-Semitism possible, and thereby led to the actions of Nazi Germany, there was a very great difference. Medieval Christians, as it were, said to Jews, "We invite and urge you to join us. If you join us, you will be free of all persecution." Sometimes they said, "If you do not accept our invitation to join us, we will be cruel to you, and expel or kill you. But do join us." The Nazis said, "You cannot join us. Whoever and whatever you are, we will kill you."

The racism of the latter part of the nineteenth century in Germany and France was a poison without antidote. By and large Holland, Britain, and the Americas resisted the infection. In these parts of the world anti-Semitism was, and has been, essentially an exasperating nuisance, something felt economically and socially (such as the barring of employment possibilities or exclusion from medical schools); it did not culminate in expulsion or death in extermination camps. But it has existed, and in varying measures still exists, at times rising and at times falling but not disappearing.

Is this surviving but limited anti-Semitism something Jews need to fear, and fear greatly, as possibly destined to result in the future in new persecutions? Or is it only something to be alert about? Individual Jews answer these questions in quite different ways. My impression is that most Jews have so abiding a faith in western democracy as to be free of genuine fear.

After World War II, a good many Christians realized that Christianity bore a heavy responsibility for Nazism and its anti-Semitism as a principal cause. Therefore, a good number of official church bodies, Vatican Council II, for example, issued public pronouncements which condemned anti-Semitism as un-Christian. Some such statements have been designed specifically to counter the charge that "the Jews" killed Jesus, and the implication that Jews, of all ages and places, share in the guilt of having caused Jesus' death. Many churches have so shaped their religious schools and the textbooks used in them to shield them from the opportunity for inculcating that kind of living anti-Semitism that the New Testament might prompt. Jews can be grateful for the extent and the earnestness of this effort.

My personal judgment is that Jews no longer have direct reason to fear Christians. It is non-Christians, or ex-Christians, in whom the folklore of anti-Semitism abides, who are a legitimate source of fear.

The Nazis, as we said above, defined a Jew as a person who had at least one Jewish grandparent. Consistent with their definition, they killed priests and nuns and ordinary Christians for the crime of such a Jewish ancestor. More than one non-Jew died in the gas chambers with a Jewish mate. A Christian who marries a Jew makes himself eligible for whatever can or will happen to Jews, and a Jew who marries a Christian exposes that person to whatever fate may await Jews. That a Jew converts to Christianity does not shield him and his children from racist anti-Semitism.

A Christian contemplating marriage to a Jew needs to ponder if he or she is prepared for what might happen to Jews. This is a reality that is for the most part quite independent of whether there is a conversion, or a flight to no religion.

Anti-Semites make no distinction among Orthodox, Conservative, Reform, or "non-Jewish" Jews. Whoever marries a Jew, even a Jew who converts to Christianity, comes to be reckoned by anti-Semites as Jewish.

I do not think American Jews are afraid. I do think they are uneasy. Can a Christian marrying a Jew withstand this uneasiness?

6

American Jews and the State of Israel

Can a Christian fully and truly understand what the State of Israel means emotionally to Jews?

A distinction should be clear respecting the partisan concern by virtually all American Jews for the State of Israel, as between theoretical Zionist ideology on the one hand, and Israel as a practical reality on the other.

Zionism is an ideology of Jewish nationalism. Its religious roots go back to the Bible and were early formulated in ancient, traditional prayers. The Holy Land, so that religious strand asserts, was divinely promised, but because of accumulated sins, Jews had been scattered into exile in all parts of the world. The ancient biblical prophets had taught that some day God would redeem and gather in the dispersed to their ancestral home; the prayer book repeated the biblical theme, adding the hope that the Messiah would soon come and usher in a miraculous return of the dispersed Jews to the Holy Land.

As a nationalist ideology, Zionism is a product of the nationalist sentiments that arose in nineteenth-century Europe. Italy sought for a unification and the establishment of a constitutional government in a movement called *risorgimento* after the conquests of Italy by Napoleon. The Papal States were then a large part of Italy. After disorders and wars with outside interveners, and advance and set-back, a united Italy was achieved in 1871. Within the then Austro-Hungarian empire there were Balkan nations which had their own nationalist hopes, many of which were realized after World War I. Thus, for well over a hundred years Europe was host to a variety of nationalisms.

In western Europe and the Americas, Jews were granted civil rights, and in ideology became nationals of the countries where they resided. In eastern Europe the hopes, arising after the French Revolution of 1789 had exerted its influence, were repeatedly dashed, and early nineteenth-century confidence that some proposed socialist solutions would bring freedom and opportunity to the impoverished and oppressed soon appeared to be baseless. Hence the view arose that Jews would achieve what they yearned for only by "self-emancipation," and this within their own national entity and in their own land. Jewish nationalism as a sentiment was thus born in Europe in the first half of the nineteenth century. Nurtured by traditional prayers, the hopes of Jews in eastern Europe were centered in a return some day to Palestine. Added to this nationalist objective, the trappings of every nation were created: a national anthem, a flag, the Hebrew language, always preserved as a written language by Jews, was revived as a spoken language to supplant Yiddish. "Pioneers" were able to found small agricultural colonies in Turkish Palestine in the nineteenth century. Zionist sentiment spread throughout the ghettos of eastern Europe.

What changed Zionism from a sentiment into a movement was the European racist anti-Semitism of the 1870s and 1880s, culminating in an event that at the time shattered much of western society. In 1894, a French Jew, Alfred Dreyfus, a captain in the army serving on its general staff, was tried by court martial on the charge of having sold secret documents to Germany. Convicted, but protesting his innocence, he was sent to Devil's Island to serve a life sentence. His brother Mathieu and a journalist, Bernard Lazare, led a campaign for a retrial because of irregularities in the court-martial procedure. Then an officer named Esterhazy was charged with being the true culprit, but was acquitted after being tried, in 1898. The head of military intelligence, a Lieutenant Colonel George Picquart, who had found the evidence against Esterhazy, was first silenced by army officials and then dismissed from the service. Esterhazy, indeed, was tried only because of public pressure on the military. But that same year the new head of army intelligence, Hubert-

Joseph Henry, confessed that he had forged the documents in order to implicate Dreyfus; arrested, Henry committed suicide in jail. Esterhazy was allowed to resign from the army and to emigrate to England.

In 1899, the highest French court of appeal ordered a new court martial for Dreyfus. Once again Dreyfus was found guilty, but now his sentence was reduced to ten years at Devil's Island. That same year a journalist-novelist named Emile Zola printed on the front page of the newspaper *Aurore* a series of paragraphs, each beginning with the words, *I accuse*, charging that Dreyfus was the victim of lies told by both military and civil authorities. For this Zola was charged with libel, then convicted, and thereupon sentenced to a year in jail; however, he had fled to England.

The Dreyfus trials and the Zola trial were part of an immense flare-up that divided France. When Dreyfus was first tried, a torrent of anti-Semitic propaganda was let loose, especially from the army. Right-wing political elements and dignitaries of the Roman Catholic Church were the leaders of the "anti-Dreyfus" elements in an issue that so divided the French people, especially after the acquittal of Esterhazy, that the country was on the brink of civil war. The second conviction of Dreyfus turned the tide, for so unpopular was the decision that a liberal-oriented government was voted into power. The influence of the military soon declined, and a separation of church and state was voted on in 1905.

The influence of the Dreyfus affair was not confined to France, but also attracted worldwide attention. Among the newspaper correspondents in Paris was a Jew, a columnist-dramatist named Theodor Herzl, the correspondent of an eminent Viennese newspaper. Appalled that in France, the cultural leader of the world and the adopted motherland of artists and thinkers, something as horrendous as the Dreyfus affair could occur, Herzl turned from indifference about Jewish affairs to preoccupation with them. In 1896, he published a book, *The Jewish State*, in which he asserted that the bad situation of Jews in Europe was bound to get even worse, and that the solution for Jews was the founding of a Jewish State by international agreement. While Herzl left to fellow Jews the choice of a territory for the proposed Jewish state, he himself favored Palestine.

His writings had great influence on Jews in eastern Europe, especially on those who had anticipated his ideas and had already created an array of "nationalist" organizations, particularly one that had been collecting funds for the purchase of land in Palestine and for settlement there. The Turks, in 1890, reversed a previous policy, and allowed Jewish settlements, but they renewed the ban on Jewish settlements a year later. This is to say, that there were movements underway well prior to Herzl's *The Jewish State*. Indeed the word *Zionism*, expressive of Jewish nationalism, had already been coined.

In 1897 Herzl convened a "World Zionist Congress" in Basel, Switzerland, and a "World Zionist Organization" was formed, and Herzl served as its President until his death in 1904.

There were diverse Jewish reactions to the formation of the World Zionist Organization. Opposition was expressed both by ultra-Orthodox and also by Reform leaders. The Orthodox opposition rested on the secular character of Zionism, for it was the Orthodox premise that a return to Palestine was up to God and not to a human organization. Reform leaders, living in western countries, denied that Jews were a nation, contending that they were a community united only by religion, and without a need for a state. But the dominant, indeed the overwhelming response of Jews was to embrace Zionism. This was especially so in eastern Europe. With the migration of Jews from eastern Europe to western countries, especially the United States, Zionist doctrines migrated with them.

East European Zionism had developed a Zionist rhetoric which spoke of Jews as a homeless nation, entitled to a national existence, and implying the personal settlement of the Zionist in the Holy Land. This rhetoric was retained by emigrants. It was brought to the United States. But the attitude to Zionism subtly shifted in the United States, not in the intensity of the support, but rather in the winnowing out of a literal, personal embrace of Jewish nationalism. There abided an unreserved sympathy for Zionism, yet without involvement in the implication of it. That is, American Zionists were Americans, of undiluted American loyalty, and without thought or intention of ever leaving these shores. One might better have spoken of "pro-Zionism" rather than of "Zionism." In brief, the rhetoric in eastern Europe was literal; in the United States, Zionism was a philanthropy, not alone to bring alleviation from hunger and thirst, but also to bring spiritual regeneration to millions of the dispossessed still caught in the eastern European ghettos. Moreover, these dispossessed were not aliens, not simply fellow Jews; they were cousins, or uncles, or sisters and brothers.

The full story must be read elsewhere; here it can only be touched upon. During World War I, on November 2, 1917, the British government issued the "Balfour Declaration," which declared that the British government "favor the establishment in Palestine of a national home for the Jewish people, and will use their best endeavors to facilitate the achievement of this object, it being clearly understood that nothing shall be done which may prejudice the civil and religious rights of existing non-Jewish communities in Palestine, or the rights and political status enjoyed by Jews in any other country." By the Balfour Declaration, Zionism achieved its first recognition by a government. Not that the Balfour Declaration pleased all Jews; anti-Zionists opposed it. Again the language of the Declaration was not precisely what Zionists had wanted, for they had preferred, instead of "*a* national home *for* the Jewish people," the wording, "*the* national home *of* the Jewish people."

In December, 1917, British forces entered Jerusalem, and in September 1918 they won a decisive military victory over the Turks. When World War I ended, and the League of Nations was formed, Palestine was entrusted to Great Britian as the "Mandatory Power" over Palestine. The Balfour Declaration was approved by other allied governments and was incorporated in the British Mandate in 1922. Zionists confidently, but mistakenly, expected the British to expedite the intent of the Balfour Declaration.

World War I had worsened the poverty of Jews in eastern Europe (and the Communist Revolution in Russia had detached Russian Jews from world Jewry). Immigration into western countries encountered rising opposition (to all immigrants, not just Jews). The settlement of Jews in Palestine was now not as much a luxury as a necessity since Jews needed to go somewhere. Jews arrived in Palestine in great numbers. They bought land, they established new agricultural collectives (kibbutzim), they built cities (Tel Aviv). But the British had detached Transjordan (later called the kingdom of Jordan) from Palestine, and there Jewish settlement was barred. The Palestinian Arabs benefited from the Jewish settlement, but Arab nationalism was rising, and sporadic disorders took place.

When the Nazis came to power in 1933, Jewish immigration to Palestine increased. But Arabs, stimulated by the Nazi and Italian fascist governments, who wished to embarrass the British, took to rioting and to guerilla warfare, and Jews increased the private military defenses they had felt compelled to organize. The British now imposed restrictions on Jewish immigration, but a considerable number of refugees came in as illegal immigrants. The British restrictions, both before World War II (1939-1945) and after, led to an intensification of activity towards an autonomous Jewish state. Large-scale military clashes took place between the Jews and the British, and between the Jews and the Arabs.

The British turned to the United Nations, which, in November 1947, recommended the partition of Palestine into two states, one Arab and one Jewish. The British then withdrew from Palestine, announcing that they would end their Mandate on May 15, 1948. On May 14, the State of Israel was proclaimed, and it was promptly recognized by govern-

ments such as the United States and Russia. Palestinian Arab
guerillas were now joined by Arab armies from Jordan, Syria,
Lebanon, Iraq, Egypt, and Saudi Arabia. The Jewish forces
were able to restrain most of such attacks, though Jordan
seized the eastern, old city of Jerusalem. On July 19, 1948,
the Security Council of the United Nations tried to enforce a
cease-fire, the second one attempted, but it did not endure.
In February, 1949, an armistice was signed by the Israelis and
the Egyptians, and in ensuing months with other countries
(Lebanon, Jordan, and Syria), but not with Iraq or Saudi
Arabia. The Israeli War of Independence, then, ended successfully in 1949. When this war had erupted in 1948, many
Arabs fled, and were settled in refugee camps in Jordan and
in the Gaza Strip, then part of Egypt. This flight of Arabs,
and the entry of over a million Jews, fleeing either from Arab
lands or coming from parts of Europe where they had survived the Nazi Holocaust, altered the character of the
population of Israeli Palestine.

War with Arab states erupted again in 1956. In 1967,
under dire threat from Nasser of Egypt and his allies, Syria
and Jordan, Israel won a quick and spectacular victory: Israel
occupied the Golan Heights that had been Syrian, the west
bank of the Jordan River, including old Jerusalem, which had
been in the kingdom of Jordan, and territories of Egypt,
including the Gaza Strip and the Sinai Peninsula up to the
Suez Canal. In October, 1973, the Syrians and Egyptians,
helped by forces from Jordan, Iraq, and Saudi Arabia,
launched a massive attack on the Day of Atonement. The
Egyptians were able to cross the Suez Canal and capture the
supposedly impregnable Bar Lev lines. After repulsing the
Syrian attack at the Golan Heights in the northeast, the
Israelis counterattacked in the southwest, and themselves
crossed the Suez Canal, and were on the verge of surrounding
and destroying the Egyptian armies. Now the United Nations
compelled a cease-fire.

The October War of 1973 ended the easy optimism on the
part of Israelis that they could inevitably deal militarily with

Arab armies. Moreover, the need of the western world for oil, in which Arab states such as Saudi Arabia were exceedingly rich, led to the political abandonment of Israel by erstwhile friendly European nations; only the Dutch and the United States rallied to the support of Israel. In the United Nations, the African and Asian states, including those which had asked for and received assistance from Israeli experts in agriculture, became a solid anti-Israel bloc. But the chief threat to Israel came from Russian manipulations and maneuvers, since Russia provides endless modern military equipment to the Arab states.

The refugee camps have constituted a grievance to Arabs. From displaced Palestinian Arabs there have emerged terrorist attacks both on Israeli settlements and on Israeli planes or ambassadorial offices throughout the world. Near the end of 1974, the United Nations welcomed to its rostrum the leader of the so-called Palestine Liberation Organization. Israel has now been denied a continuing membership in UNESCO; American Jews were once ardent supporters of the United Nations but this is no longer so.

The story of Israel is not that of its wars. It is the story of arid land reclaimed and of fertile agriculture, of lives regenerated after concentration camps, of universities and of symphony orchestras, and of poets and artists. The racists had spoken of Semites as an inferior people; it was a lie, and the achievements of Jews have proven it to be a lie. Israel to American Jews represents the capacity of harassed and broken Jews to rebuild their lives, which is a unique demonstration of the sturdiness of the human spirit.

Pride in Israel's cultural achievements, pride in her self-reliance, and, above all, her unremitting concern for fellow Jews everywhere are epitomized for us in the State of Israel.

As American Jews we are not Israelis. We consider America our home and gladly bind our destiny to it. Christians will find extremes of opinion concerning Israel among Jews. One extreme is represented by a handful among us who for whatever reason conceive the State of Israel as a development that should never have occurred, regarding the State of Israel as something of a threat to personal security, as if it casts doubt on the legitimacy of American citizenship and loyalty. A few Jews even hate Israel; most, though, are apprehensive about the impingement of Israel on them.

Another extreme is a much larger group whose preoccupations and dedications are to the State of Israel to the exclusion of all else. Such people may otherwise shun all other Jewish activities, including synagogue attendance and religious observance in the home. Such people practically eat, breathe, and sleep Israel, and they are prone to be personally affronted by any enthusiasm for Israel that is in any way less than their own. Any criticism of policies or actions of the State of Israel is to them the ultimate in blasphemy.

But it is not Israel the State or its government that concerns most of us. The state and its government matter only insofar as the well-being of Jews is concerned. Israelis are not faceless people to us. They are literally our brothers and cousins, and we care about them. We want our fellow Jews in Israel to have peace, to have some freedom from want. We react, of course, to terrorism. Yet our concern for our fellow Jews in no sense prompts us to hate Arabs. What we long for is for Israel to live in affirmative harmony with her Arab neighbors.

In 1967 we were possibly overoptimistic at Israel's quick and decisive military victory, and the feeling that Israel could handle any military threat. Today, after the Yom Kippur War of 1973, the future of Israel seems dark. We are greatly worried, perhaps overly so. We wonder if peace will be maintained; we wonder if Israel can afford further wars, even victorious ones. We wonder if Israel—it is something we shudder to think about and we seldom put into words—were to lose a war with Arab neighbors, would its people be massacred? Would they really be driven into the sea, as Nasser of Egypt threatened to do in 1967?

We are uneasy. More uneasy about what lies ahead in the future for the Jews in Israel than about what lies ahead for us here.

The history of Zionism and of Israel has been dotted with names of Christian Zionists, proponents and friends of the purposes and goals of Zionism. Once the State of Israel was established, one segment of Christendom, conservative Protestantism, embraced the state with warmth and even enthusiasm, seeing it as consistent with their views of biblical prophecy. From a totally different perspective, some liberal Protestants expressed comparable support. So, too, did some important Catholic clergymen.

Under Pope Paul VI, however, opposition to the State of Israel has varied and the Vatican has scarcely uttered a sympathetic word. Jews are not happy about this.

Yet even greater unhappiness is the result of antagonism to the State of Israel of liberal Protestants. It was from liberal Protestants especially that Jews expected both understanding and some warm concern. Men of consequence and high position in the liberal Protestant world have written about Israel in ways that have been no less than scurrilous. Most American Jews had felt an affinity with liberal Protestants, rather than with conservatives or fundamentalists, and they had joined with liberal Protestants in such enterprises as integration, proper housing, and social welfare. Whether justly or not, many Jews feel that liberal Christians, as it were, deluded and betrayed Jews, and some Jews are very bitter about this.

Here are two statements which are in close juxtaposition to each other. First, to criticize Israel is the right of every free man, and a criticism of Israel, its policies, and actions is by no means a word or act of anti-Semitism. Second, some Christians, since anti-Semitism is currently socially disapproved, couch their anti-Semitism in terms of anti-Israel statements.

Much of our organized Jewish philanthropy is directed towards Israel. But we have also our American indigent poor, our local hospitals, a concern for Jews overseas in lands apart from Israel. We have no dearth of charitable organizations, which support schools and rabbinic academies overseas. Jews ordinarily join virtually all such organizations, but activity beyond the payment of dues is what marks the special interest of particular Jews. Whatever a person's bent might be, he or she can be assured that there is at least one Jewish organization to satisfy it; usually there are at least two!

7

The Children's Religious Education and Identification

We have already touched on the question whether the children will be raised as Christians, as Jews, or as nothing. To what extent can the sociological factor be separated from the religious one? Does the toleration of a person for the spouse's religion extend to having the children raised in that religion? The honest answer in many cases is no.

The reason, of course, lies in the very nature of the historic relations. If a Christian holds the traditional view that Judaism is a religion inferior to Christianity, or a Jew that Christianity is an inferior religion, he can scarcely welcome his child's being reared in what is inferior, for we all want the best for our children. I have been told that a certain Christian (after a drink or two) said, "I don't mind my daughter marrying a damn Jew, but I'll be damned if I'll put up with my grandchildren being raised as Jews." I have personally heard a Jew say, "I don't mind my son marrying a Christian, but I'll be damned if I'll put up with my own grandchild calling me a 'Christ-killer.' " To the extent that the parents (as distinct from the grandparents) retain vestiges of such anxieties or scorns, the problem of what to do with the children is a most crucial one, and one which presents the greatest of all the dangers to a successful marriage.

One must distinguish between the attitudes of the more thoughtful and discerning people for whom all religions have validity, being only different from each other, and not subject to words such as *better* and *worse*, and the attitudes of people who, without necessarily saying so, think their own either the only true religion and all others false, or at least not quite as true as their own.

It is a fact that Jews regard fellow Jews, and Christians fellow Christians, as finer people. Or, if not precisely finer, there is a closer affinity between fellow Jews as there is between fellow Christians. Persons within one fellowship tend to look at others as "aliens." Such sentiments are, of course, not confined to Jews and Christians; Jews of one national background can feel that Jews of a different one are also alien; similarly, Protestants and Catholics can regard each other as aliens.

What does a Christian perceive in a child being raised as a Jew? That child is presumably reared in an atmosphere marked by exclusivism. The child is expected not to recite the Lord's Prayer, not to observe Easter or Christmas, and is cut off from that which is possibly precious to his parent. In place of the familiar, the child is raised with the unfamiliar, with a different array of holy days, and different perceptions of many things. If the child is sent to a Jewish religious school, he is taught Hebrew, or at least Hebrew phrases, and reared to be loyal to a set of symbols totally diverse from one's parent. At a religious school he will be taught, or influenced to think, that the Jewish people constitute an ongoing community that is self-contained, whose needs, purposes, and preoccupations cut him off from his Christian parent's community entirely. To rear one's child to be a Jew is in effect to cut him off from Christianity.

The child reared in a Jewish school will never be exposed to sacred books with anti-Christian passages. He may be exposed to passages in the Hebrew Bible that pour scorn on Canaanites, or on ancient Gentiles, and some of this, in the hands of narrow teachers, can be interpreted as including Christians too. Surely the child in a Jewish religious school will get some smattering of the persecutions which Christian churches subjected Jews to in the Middle Ages, and absorb a resentment of these. He may also in some schools be exposed to an unbecoming scorn of his parent's beliefs and practices, and that scorn can be debilitating to the parent when it chances to be conveyed to him. The child in a Jewish school will never be taught to hate Christians. But Jewish religious schools are only in the smallest number completely free of innuendoes of an anti-Christian timber.

The Christian child of a Jewish parent goes through a comparable set of experiences, with the specific aspects varying from one Christian religious school to another. He will be expected to repeat prayers which his parent has been reared to regard as inappropriate or else futile, to recite a creed his parent does not believe in; all this is pretty much the opposite number of what the Jewish child of a Christian parent experiences.

There is, though, the additional and inescapable factor, that Jews and Judaism figure in Christian Scripture, as we have mentioned above. It is here that the possibility of very great friction can arise. Will the Jewish parent tolerate his Christian offspring learning a Gospel lesson, the essence of which is to portray the Jews of Jesus' time as hypocrites or villains or bloodthirsty? If he accompanies his child to a Christian worship service, will he be content to hear passages read from the pulpit that scorn not only ancient Jews but Judaism as a wrong religion, wondrously superseded by Christianity? If the parent has been reared to love the Torah, how will he respond to passages in the Epistles of Paul that proclaim its inadequacy and nullification?

It must be clearly stated that many a modern Christian is completely free of the anti-Judaism and anti-Jewish sentiments found in Christian Scripture. The Christian Scriptures, though, are not, and cannot, be freed of such passages. Many a modern church has made earnest, strenuous efforts to exclude from its church school such textbooks which make direct reference to anti-Jewish passages in the New Testament. If there exists the will to do so, the New Testament can be taught with disciplined abstention from rehearsing its anti-Jewish tones, which is the case in some churches.

But this is by no means the case in all churches. If a Jew marries a Christian of a fundamentalist church and his child is reared as a Christian, he should expect his child to be taught that the New Testament is the Word of God. He should expect the anti-Jewish passages to be taught to his child. One should remember that the New Testament is more than just its anti-Jewish passages, and that the affirmative values outnumber and outweigh the anti-Jewish; perhaps the affirmative can be an antidote. Indeed, a frequent approach on the part of conservative Protestants is to regard the Jews of the New Testament not as the Jewish people but as the wicked members of the Christian community.

To what extent does a child in these circumstances encounter anomalies? That is, do the playmates of a child of an intermarriage fully accept such a youngster as one of their own? So far as I know, they do. Of course, if a child with a characteristic name like Finkelstein or Goldberg describes himself, in all correctness, as a Christian, or a McGillicuddy as a Jew, some inevitable confusion of fun-poking can arise. Even if this is mostly of little consequence, it can occasionally be painful.

Children can also be victims of the foibles and meanness of people. There are Jews who will regard the child of a Christian as a Christian despite his being reared as a Jew. To an even greater extent, a Jew in such circumstances often continues to be regarded as a Jew, and not as an authentic Christian. There is a long history to support this phenomenon. Both Benjamin Disraeli and Karl Marx were born Christian, though of Jewish parents; they were customarily referred to throughout their careers as Jews, and Disraeli in Parliament was taunted as such.

Surely children need to be prepared, if not for ugly experiences, at least for puzzling or painful ones. And surely the parents need to be alert.

But it will not do for an intermarrying couple to abstain from the fullest consideration of what they will do long before the children come. Surely they ought to give the matter thoughtful attention even before the wedding.

Reaching a decision is often exceedingly difficult, and full frankness is elusive. Even when there is the fullest possible open exchange of opinions and an advance agreement reached, the caution needs to be expressed that people can decide things in good faith and then a change of minds can occur (and lead to the charge of bad faith).

When an upsetting change of mind occurs, it can appear both unexpected and mystifying to the spouse, for the point of departure for the change can be completely outside that spouse's ken, with the other party unable to articulate the basis for the change. Aroused loyalties, once dormant and always tacit, occasion such changes.

Perhaps even worse than the tension that an expressed change of mind occasions is the unexpressed but deeply felt wish for a change. Burning inner resentment can be an infection that, like a cancer, spreads throughout the vital organs. A couple ought periodically to review their decision about the children, querying each other to discover if they remain satisfied with it. And should their child report some incident to them, then it is essential for the couple to have an unrestrained exchange with each other not only about the incident, but to what extent, if any, the incident impinges on the decision they have made.

If the intermarrying couple are able to reach the fullest understanding, can this understanding be conveyed to their children? At what age? In what circumstances?

Some parents I know of raise their children not as Christians or as Jews, but as both. Perhaps that works. But do the children understand?

Children are resilient and it is easy to attribute to them problems which are only the projections of parents' concerns. This seems to me a distinct possibility. But is not such projection of itself a reflection of parental disquiet? And can the parents in some way forefend against involuntarily imposing on children the disquiet that they mistakenly thought they would never feel?

One Jewish conviction, which Christians should be aware of, is that the child of a Jew is going to be regarded as a Jew, despite conversion. Therefore, so the line of reasoning runs, since the child is going to be regarded as a Jew, he might as well be Jewish, and not undergo conversion to Christianity.

This attitude is not so much the set of a mind or of reason, but an emotional syndrome, and a reasonable counter-approach is possibly ineffective. I have an impression that Christians can ordinarily not fathom the whys and wherefores of this syndrome among Jews. It may well be only a rationalization for the Jewish parent's determination that the child remain Jewish; in any case it is an attitude that exists.

What social experience awaits the child when he or she is old enough to date? Local circumstances can differ. If the setting is one in which there are Jewish clubs, or Jewish college fraternities and sororities, then the greatest likelihood exists that, even reared as a Christian, the child will live his social life within the Jewish community. Let a Christian be assured that such a social life is not without its attractions. It is not a fate worse than death. To the contrary, it can be quite pleasant.

Pleasant, indeed, unless the child, for whatever reason, attaches some stigma to the Jewish social life. How pitiable it is for a Christian child to be in effect an unwilling Jew, whom society pushes into the Jewish community!

If the local setting is different, the experience of a child of intermarriage who is reared as a Christian can be relatively free from such experience. But let the parents, even before they are parents, try to understand what their children may experience. Things may be much harder for the children than for the parents.

8

Asset or Liability

The two traditions are rich in their culture of literature, music, art, and philosophy. Will an intermarrying couple find enrichment in their diversity or background? Or will they feel so constrained to neutrality that their intermarriage in effect robs them of both legacies?

The fact needs to be recognized that some marriages, which are not intermarriages, are devoid of depth and of authentic and lasting love, and intermarriages can also be so blemished.

If both parties to a marriage come to some inner security in their personal religion (or lack of it), they ought to reach some common understanding that the accumulated culture of religions is not the same as a worship service or a creed. In a context in which a couple enjoy together a symphony or an art exhibit, they ought not deny themselves the esthetic creations which emerge from the religious traditions. There is a sense in which music such as Bach's *B Minor Mass* and Bernstein's *Jeremiah Symphony* are part of modern culture and have a potential universal appeal, such as Bach to non-Christians and Bernstein to non-Jews. Even if one grants that a Christian will derive more from the *B Minor Mass* than a Jew, or a Jew more from the *Jeremiah Symphony* than a Christian, there is nevertheless a good possibility of a common delight. Just as one does not need to be an Italian to relish the deft satire and skillful music in the Puccini opera *Gianni Schichi*, so a Jew can feel free to respond to medieval English Christmas carols or a Christian to the Yiddish song, "A Cantor for the Sabbath." In the theater, we are usually prepared to suspend our rational faculties, and, in a play such as *Harvey,* accept the premise that an unseen rabbit six foot tall is an actual character in the drama, or that in *Hamlet* the father's ghost can talk to his son. Surely we should be able to suspend our theological disbeliefs respecting the culture of a religion not our own.

If a couple is so extreme and so rigid, for the sake of domestic peace, as to feel the need for self-deprivation, then surely something is amiss in the relationship, and surely the marriage is impoverished.

I began above with the premise that the partners have come to some inner security. Unless this is the case, there is danger that the line of demarcation between sectarian religious observance and the universal human appeal of religious culture will be blurred. In such cases, a Jew can feel that to listen to Handel's *Messiah* is the same as taking communion in a church service, or for a Christian to attend a performance of the Ernest Bloch *Sacred Service* is equivalent to a tacit profession of Judaism. Undoubtedly there are people of this kind in both communities, whose dissent from the religion not their own prompts them to rigorous exclusions. Do such people enrich themselves, or do they impoverish themselves?

Where does a different kind of person draw the line between the narrowly religious, which in conscience he cannot accept, and the broader culture which he can? I know no formula beyond mutual, solicitous consultation or common sense. There are Jews who regard a Christmas tree as the highest form of professing the Christian faith, and Christians who would consider foregoing a Christmas tree as the extreme self-sacrifice. It is to be doubted that accurate knowledge of the relatively late and pagan origin of the Christmas tree is in any way influential. I suppose that certain selective symbols carry an inordinate weight for some people. Only in these terms do I understand the Cross or Star of David serving as jewelry, being fashioned into a necklace, or into a tiepin. The Christian wife who wears a cross around her neck to a synagogue service should be aware that she is thereby proclaiming a bit too loudly that she is not religiously allied with her husband, and that there can be Jews who would regard this sort of thing as in bad taste. In recent times the ancient Jewish custom of putting a *mezzuzah* on the doorpost of a house has been broadly revived after almost disappearing. The mezzuzah is a container into which a small, rolled piece of parchment is put, containing passages from the Book of Deuteronomy, including "Hear, O Israel, the Lord our God, the Lord is One" (6:4). Recently artisans have fashioned elegant and very often beautiful mezzuzahs of silver. The mezzuzah as a symbol proclaims that the home is a Jewish one. Can it be used if the home isn't completely Jewish?

If it is right that certain specific symbols, despite whatever artistry is involved in their making, both gratify and offend, then they need to be avoided, for if no reciprocal understanding exists about them, they will appear to represent unwilling religious concessions.

But quite apart from these symbols which have gained associations of special emphasis and force, and thereby can constitute problems, there exists a wide and broad range of cultural creations that can reasonably be shared. To forego these could be a pity. The challenge, then, is how they can be fitted into an intermarriage harmoniously. It seems to me more desirable to discover how to use them than simply to shun them completely. There is a world of difference between the Mozart or Verdi *Requiems* and recurrent presentations of a so-called passion play, a costumed presentation of the last days of Jesus. One such play was presented in my city a few years ago, with the novelty that its Jesus was a black and the villainous Jews were white. The Jewish community included fearful individuals whose anxiety—a real anxiety—was that through the play, the audience would immediately become a mob which would work physical harm, if not on Jews, then on the business establishments of Jews. (There was no such sequel.)

The basic question is whether the parties to an intermarriage are to stifle the possible wealth of the background of each, or enrich each other. The answers lie in the reciprocal understanding of both parties to such questions. But the first step is the common premise that both backgrounds do possess facets of admirable culture that can be shared in such a way as to abstain from offending one's spouse's theological sensibilities. The partners ought to be enriched by their marriage to each other. Such enrichment is a distinct possibility in an intermarriage. The common quest, then, ought to be that the difference in backgrounds should provide enrichment.

An Epilogue for Christians

The presentation of history and theology, of dangers and pitfalls, and affirmative opportunities, now lies behind us. Perhaps I have in some ways succeeded in providing a fair and balanced presentation.

The following words are addressed to Christians, not to Jews: What can await you if you conclude that you want to become Jewish?

Will you be hospitably received? By most of us Jews, yes. Will there be some who will not succeed in stifling or concealing some inhospitality? I am afraid so. Is such possible inhospitality a reason for not becoming Jewish? Not at all.

Will you at times feel strange? Yes. But progressively less and less so.

How have other converts to Judaism fared respecting the treatment accorded to them by Jews? I suppose that some have momentarily fared ill. Our ancient documents prescribed that our initial response to a would-be convert is to deter him, to make him aware of the sufferings that Jews have gone through, and only thereafter to receive him. Perhaps among some of us a recollection of the injunction to deter becomes altered into overtones of unwelcome. But overwhelmingly we receive a convert with full warmth and a full welcome. We do this without making any undue fuss over the convert. He becomes one of us quietly. In the course of time we respond to him in terms of his personality and characteristics. We respond to him for what he is, not for the accident of his birth.

As mentioned above, the ancient documents, in the interest of an assurance that the would-be convert be prompted by a pure motive, prohibit conversion in connection with a marriage. I personally must dissent from this prohibition. I can readily understand conversion connected with a marriage; in all candor, I have anxieties about conversions not so connected. Is such a potential convert a fully-balanced individual? In view of the range of religious possibilities within Christendom, why should a person of Christian background, not contemplating marrying a Jew, search outside Christianity for his religious satisfactions? I have too high a respect for Christianity to be willing to acquiesce in the implication that it is a deficient or invalid religion. Yet perhaps a would-be convert to Judaism has glimpsed something that has irresistably attracted him; if such a person has a rational basis for wishing to be Jewish, that is fine. I would think that mental stability ought to be a requisite factor. I have known converts to Judaism unconnected with a wedding whom I have been able to understand, and to whose conversions I could have assented. But beyond such isolated individual instances, I remain anxious, for I do not know how to cope with psychological syndromes which I do not and cannot fully grasp.

But conversion in connection with a marriage is so commonsense a matter that I have no difficulty in understanding it.

The Book of Ruth tells of a Moabite girl who became a Jewess. She is portrayed as speaking these words to her mother-in-law Naomi: "Do not persuade me to cut myself off from you. Where you go, I will go. Where you live, I will live. Your people are my people, your God my God. Where you die, let me die, and there be buried . . ."

A Christian earnestly able to speak in this kind of way seems to me deserving of the warmest reception by us Jews. I do not speak for others, but for me such a declaration is a sufficient form of conversion. If someone is willing without reservation to throw in his or her lot with the intended, and with us Jews, I can and would gladly welcome him or her.

Many, many centuries ago, Jews maintained an active missionary movement, a fact known only to scholars. In recent centuries Jews have had neither the will nor the capacity to seek proselytes. In recent decades some individual Jews have proposed the adoption of an active missionary movement to recruit converts. Perhaps there is merit in the thought, for Jews ought reasonably share with others the heritage they consider precious. Yet as I have thought about this (and done so most infrequently) it has seemed to me that proselytes, if sought, should be sought from among those devoid of religion. I see no purpose or gain in trying and succeeding in weaning Christians away from Christianity.

To abstain from seeking proselytes is surely different from receiving them when they come on their own. I for one am always prepared to find room in Judaism for people who come voluntarily. We Jews have no exclusive monopoly on good people. If good people from the outside wish to join with us, by all means let them do so.

What can we Jews do for and with such people? We can let them share our good heritage. We Jews, warts and all, are a good people, and in some ways we can say we have been a gifted people. We cannot know what lies ahead for us from the outside, though I personally have no fear. From the inside we can offer a certain vigor, a certain wisdom, a certain high measure of human aspiration, and a high devotion to what is worthy.

We would want a Jew who in earnestness becomes a Christian to fare well in that good heritage.

We can assure anyone who becomes a Jew that we will share our goodness and our gifts.

Suggested Readings

The Spirit of Protestantism by Robert McAfee Brown (New York: Oxford University Press, 1961).

The Protestant Faith by George W. Forell (Philadelphia: Fortress Press, 1975).

The Meaning of Judaism by Roland Gittelsohn (New York: World Publishing Company, 1970).

His Many Mansions by Rulon S. Howells (New York: World Publishing Company, 1972).

Guide to Jewish Holy Days by Hayyim Schauss (New York: Schocken Books, 1962).

Basic Judaism by Milton Steinberg (New York: Harcourt Brace and World, 1947).

The Protestant Era by Paul J. Tillich, James Luther Adams, trans. (Chicago: University of Chicago Press, 1957).

Introducing Contemporary Catholicism by Theodore Westow (Philadelphia: Westminster Press, 1967).